The
True History
of
Master Fard Muhammad

By

Elijah Muhammad
Messenger of Allah

Compiled & Edited By
Nasir Makr Hakim
Founder,
Secretarius MEMPS Ministries

Published by
Secretarius MEMPS Ministries
111 E Dunlap Ave, Ste 1-217
Phoenix, Arizona 85020-7802
Phone & Fax 602 466-7347
Email: secmemps@gmail.com
Web: www.memps.com

THE TRUE HISTORY OF MASTER FARD MUHAMMAD

Copyright © 1996
Secretarius Publications
Second Edition

ISBN10 # 1-884855-78-4
EAN13 978-1-884855-78-8

Printed in the United States of America

Acknowledgment

In the Name of Allah, Who came in the person of Master Fard Muhammad, to Whom all praise is forever due, the Lord of All the Worlds, and in the Name of His Last and Greatest Messenger, the Most Humble and Honorable Elijah Muhammad.

The making of this book was a task made much easier by the assistance of Sister Rose Hakim, my wife and Executive Secretary, Secretarius MEMPS. Her detailed work pertaining to the overall supervision of operations afforded valuable time for the start to completion of this work. I am very gratified with the work of my daughter, Sister Dur're Shahwar Aqueela bint Hakim, who transcribed the audio and video tapes necessary for this book. Thanks to Brother Minister David Pasha, Minister of Elijah Muhammad, for his introduction, proof reading, constructive insight and valuable advice. Thanks to my son, Brother Taqqee Aamil Hakim, for his maintenance of our database and grammar and spell checking. I want to extend my thanks my two sons, Junaid Shafeeq and Khalfani Hassan, for their hard work and sacrifice of some of their childhood for a potentially better adulthood. Lastly, many heartfelt thanks to those of you who support our efforts by contributing items by Messenger Elijah Muhammad to us.

I pray that Allah, Master Fard Muhammad, is pleased with our intent and the product. We try very hard to represent the Messenger's representation of Him in the highest scholarly manner possible.

I desire, if it pleases Allah, to compile another book from the Messenger's works, which goes specifically into an analytical view of the Messengership of Elijah Muhammad, Messenger of Allah. I pray Allah (God), Who came in the person of Master Fard Muhammad, that I have competent help in preparing this book as well. Thanks to all who helped in preparing this book.

Nasir Makr Hakim,
Minister of Elijah Muhammad,
Messenger of Allah

Dedication

This book is dedicated to those who are "Products of the
Word," who, having not seen, yet believe and are doers
of the Word and not hearers only.
This book is also dedicated
to those who can walk
and work by belief
in the word and
not by the sight
of personality.

Table of Contents

Acknowledgment iii

Dedication v

Table of Contents vi

Introduction vii

Forward xiv

The Authority To Be An Authority xxxv

A Child Born In Heaven Chapter 1 1

The Coming of The Son of Man Chapter 2 23

   The Mystery Of Hiram The Widow's Son 42

   "Christian Ministry of Freemasonry" 43

   "The Fez" 44

The Coming of The Great Mahdi Chapter 3 45

How To Understand Jesus Chapter 4 67

A Saviour Is Born Chapter 5 89

That Which You Should Know – Interpretation of Signs
Chapter 6 113

Endnotes 122

~ ~ ~ ~ ~

Introduction

by Minister David Pasha

This book is another in the series of re-publications of the authentic works of the Honorable Elijah Muhammad, the last Messenger of Allah. This honored work has been embarked on by Minister Nasir Makr Hakim, founder and the staff of Messenger of Elijah Muhammad Propagation Society (MEMPS). The avowed principles of MEMPS in doing "the much needed work of getting His (The Messenger's) words out" is once again epitomized in this rendering.

The direct intended beneficiary of this work is that body of black people - in America in particular and the world in general - who have not had access to the literature re-published herein. Incidental beneficiaries are Believers in Islam as taught by The Honorable Elijah Muhammad and anyone who does not have a source for the clear, unabridged words of The Messenger which are undiluted, mixed and tampered with in any form.

This, admittedly, is a labor by Believers who are disciples of The Honorable Elijah Muhammad. The Messenger repeatedly outlines the parameter of His Mission as being "the clear delivery of the Message." The Founder of MEMPS - like the traditional history version of the Apostle Paul as relates to the Jesus of 2,000 years ago - was not privy to a personal relationship with The Messenger during His daily public ministry among us. But, like Paul after the departure of His Leader and Teacher from public life, he has become fascinated with the power of the Message and has accepted it with full

vii

faith in the truth of it. Like Paul, he has accepted the challenge of getting this Message to the direct intended beneficiaries aforesaid. Like Paul, his faith has the substance that he will one day be blessed to see the divine fulfillment of God's Promise. Inherent in that faith is the understanding of the Principle of The Messenger's teachings that there is no physical life after physical death. Therefore, it necessarily follows that the stated fulfillment will take place during our lifetime.

The pattern of The Messenger, in His personally supervised re-publication of His works, i.e. "Supreme Wisdom, Vol. #I & #II, "Message to the Black Man in America," "How to Eat to Live, Vol.#I & #II," "The Fall of America," and "Our Saviour Has Arrived," has been followed as much as practical.

Scholarly footnotes are used throughout the work so that the reader can expand on his or her research if such is desired. Careful attention has been given to reporting what The Messenger said exactly as he said it.

In "Can One Explain What One Doesn't Understand," the MEMPS founder expands on the Divine Axiom given to us by The Messenger that "one cannot say, act or do with reference to that which he does not have the knowledge of." He applies the Axiom to confused and contradictory dynamics that mark the efforts of the uninformed as to, and the enemies of, the truth which God, in The Person of Master Fard Muhammad, revealed to The Honorable Elijah Muhammad. The paper trail of these dynamics is well documented While both this offering and the subsequent "The Authority to Be an Authority" are essentially essays by Minister Hakim, he interlaces his witness bearing with the guidance and lessons from his Leader and Teacher.

The chapter "A Child Born in Heaven" is the transcript of the very comprehensive teaching on the History of Master Fard Muhammad by The Messenger Himself on Saviour's Day 1958.

In the chapter "The Son of Man," the Messenger re-published from several sources - reveals some of the hidden science in the rituals practiced in the white man's secret societies known as: 1) Masonry; 2) Higher Masonry and 3) Muslim Shriners.

Many black men and women in America have spent large sums of money joining the free and accepted Masonic Order Fraternity and the female affiliate, The Order of the Eastern Star.

Prior to becoming a follower of The Honorable Elijah Muhammad, this writer was inducted into "The Blue House" of The Prince Hall affiliated Masonic Order. Prince Hall, a late 18th century black man, is generally accepted as the founder of BLACK free masonry in the United States. The events giving rise to this acceptance are variously reported as taking place sometime between 1775 & 1787. Chronologically, according to Masonic tradition, the charter issued by the British Grand Lodge made the lodge of Hall and his black colleagues the premier Masonic order in America, black or white.

Messenger Muhammad's teachings as to the nature and position of the slavemasters and their children is borne out in that one dynamic. White Masonic lodges do not recognize any black Masonic lodges as being legitimate. They scorn the black Masonic community as being "clandestine" work, i.e. irregular and unauthorized.

THE TRUE HISTORY OF MASTER FARD MUHAMMAD

The Messenger delineates how in this society, the history of our people, including our glorious pre-slavery past, our enslavement and the coming of Master Fard Muhammad, to Whom praise is due forever, is set forth, if, but understood.

In the chapter "The Coming of The Mahdi", The Messenger goes into details on a subject that is replete throughout His teaching. We have learned that the central figure of religious thought and organization in Western Civilization has been "colored" by the European Representatives who have used His name falsely to bring into subjection nine-tenths of the total population of the planet Earth.

Just as the true history of Master Fard Muhammad and His Lost Found People, (we the so-called American Negroes), has been hidden under the symbolism of free Masonry, so Messenger Muhammad teaches us, has the same history been hidden under the way European scholars and scientists have presented Jesus to the world. The key to the deceit is to make the masses think that events which were prophesied for the past 6,000 years - to take place in the last days of the rule of the wicked white, European based Western Civilization which is epitomized in the United States of America - all took place 2,000 years ago.

Europeans, says God to us through His Messenger, also wrote themselves into roles that really describe the Lost People of God, who have been chosen - because of the wisdom of their fore-fathers and the prolonged suffering of their progenitors - as the base for the Divine order that is being ushered in by Master Fard Muhammad, to Whom praise is due forever, which is referred to in scripture as the Kingdom of Heaven and the Hereafter, inter alia.

The constant thesis of the Theology - from God, to The Messenger, to the Black people of America in particular, to the Black people of the world in general, and even to the world at large - is that the picture painted of Jesus of Nazareth by traditional Western sources is based on contrived lies and deception. This basis has projected a series of mistruths into a world-wide acceptance of a myth or legend that is not grounded in truth, i.e. the Jesus, His life and death and its significance, especially to the so-called American Negroes.

As time goes on and research intensifies, that which God taught His Messenger is repeatedly borne out as the truth. The controversial nature of the truth and of the man chosen to deliver it to the contrary notwithstanding, scholars and scientists in the wisest quarters are bearing witness to the truth of Messenger Muhammad's revelation from God in the Person of Master Fard Muhammad, to Whom praise is due forever.

The Messenger, over the years, has told us that the wise men of the East and the West were aware that He was teaching the truth. He said that as the time of the literal end draws nearer, these secret admissions would become public.

Recent developments in several quarters bear witness to the dynamics that The Messenger has fore-armed us with reference to a syndicated story, originating with the Los Angeles Times in late October of 1995, noted that the semi-annual meeting of a group of Liberal Bible scholars, known as the Jesus Seminar, took place in Santa Rosa, California. This group of scholars are already on record contending that few historical details of the death of Jesus are reliable.

The report goes on to say that scholarly debates over "Who was Jesus?" are of long standing. However, as The Messenger teaches, academic decorum has always frowned on taking the subject beyond classrooms, erudite journals and scholarly meetings.

Further bearing witness to The Messenger's Divine Predictions, one Catholic scholar, John Dominic Crossan, who does not subscribe to the traditional Jesus myths, says "what is different now is that we are inviting ordinary people on the cutting edge of the debate."

Burton Mack, of the School of Theology at Claremont, California, reputedly, has written a book which contends, with many other scholarly treatises, that traditional Christianity is a product of layers of myth and story telling by early Christian writers after the death of the Jesus born in Palestine 2,000 years ago.

A conclave of Western scholars, whose orientation is steeped in traditional Christian lore, has, over the last 10 years, whittled away at the biblical account of the life of the Jesus of 2,000 years ago. The consensus of position is that 82 percent of His reputed words are rejected as not being His. This consensus also dismisses the Resurrection as myth.

The Messenger for over 60 years has been teaching that approximately 75 percent of the traditional history of Jesus is not literally related to the historical Jesus, but is encouched in symbolism that prophetically relates to Master Fard

Muhammad, His birth, His work of finding His People, raising His Last Messenger, The Last Messenger's work and the Redemption of the Mahdi's People. These subjects are epitomized in the aforementioned chapter.

The consequence of this undertaking is: 1) to introduce many to the 60 year plus consistency of the teachings of God's Last Messenger to us; 2) to remind many who have been conversant with these teachings; and 3) to bear witness that the truth and power of the Messenger's mission is more significant today than ever as we near the literal climax of that mission.

* David Pasha; A.B. LL. B., J D

---

* Formerly: Assistant Attorney General State of Ohio and Member of Legal Division of The Proctor & Gamble Co.

Appointed by Messenger Muhammad As House Counsel for Muhammad's Temples of The Holy Temple of Islam; November, 1965, and Minister June, 1966.

Currently: C.E.O. of Early Childhood Development Institute and The African American Acculturation Association.

Forward

Can One Teach What One Does Not Know?

How can one teach the people to know that which one does not know their self? Is it not true that to teach the people one way or the other, without knowledge, about anything, one can be charged with lying to the people? One cannot teach that which one does not know!

It is the burden of the scientist to factually discover, describe, explain and predict according to real propositions or laws. As well, the extent to which a scientist comprehends the laws or principles governing the facts he or she has under study, is the gauge of his or her ability to determine the exact nature and function of what's being studied. Surely, the capacity to understand may be greater than the demonstrated ability to explain, but the mastery to explain anything cannot go beyond one's insight into the laws and principles governing the thing.

The explanation of any reality depends on, and can be no better than, our understanding of that reality. Fundamental to understanding is knowledge. Flaws in knowledge must result in flaws in understanding. Such flaws will always be mirrored in our explanations of reality. This defective frame of mind filters what we see, how we see things and why we see things, which rules our actions.

It is well known that the world in which we live does not base its findings exclusively on reality or natural laws. One great

xiv

indictment of "this world" is manifested through how it goes about proving conclusions. The scientists are constantly testing their hands at determining patterns, predicting those patterns, and modifying them for the eventual purpose of controlling them. If they "knew" or had concrete knowledge, studying them wouldn't be necessary.

They don't know, which is why "theories" are such a fundamental part of Western World thought. A theory is systematically organized knowledge applicable in a relatively wide variety of circumstances, especially a system of assumptions, "accepted" principles, and rules of procedure devised to analyze, predict, or otherwise "explain" the nature or behavior of a specified set of phenomena. Also, theory is an assumption or guess based on limited knowledge or information.

Living under the rule of other than our own kind and self for the past 6000 years has brought much misunderstanding, much not knowing and many theories that have been used in many places and the people have taken theories that have been used in many places. A theory is not true until it has been proven to be true.[1]

It is no coincidence that earning the highest educational degree in the Western World, in most cases, requires writing a dissertation, which is a proposition maintained by argument, or a hypothetical proposition, especially one put forth for the sake of argument or one to be accepted without proof. When there is no proof, then sometimes, more often than not, the force of repetition stands with said writers as the equivalent of proof. To repeat certain statements while ignoring rebutting facts, is a sure method of carrying convictions to the minds of thousands.

They play upon the mob psychology and produce the desired effect.

When it comes to the true history of Master Fard Muhammad, Messenger Elijah Muhammad and the Nation of Islam, in general, the above method has and is being used one hundred percent. The media engages in spreading lies and fabrications through the forms of newspapers, magazines, books, news casting by radio and television. This is not just being done by whites; however, blacks have and are doing their fair share.

The popular course of writing against the Nation of Islam, more particularly, Master Fard Muhammad is this: 1) initial writers publish works which include statements of suggestion or insinuation; 2) This possibility is then transformed into a theory with follow-up works and additional media sources; 3) further follow-ups try to make a fact out of the theory. 4) Based on 1, 2, 3, above, what started as an ill-intended desire, eventually is converted, in 4 or 5 transfigurations, to a so-called "well established fact."

Take for example, the various points of view passed down through history, which attempt to "explain" the origin of Master Fard Muhammad and the Nation of Islam. The obvious variations and often contradictions manifest a gross indictment of ignorance. Most of the writing springs from the 1930's and lays a foundation for the various perpetuated theories still alive in these modern times.

During the Great Depression, the urban ghettos of the northern United States were fertile ground for the development of new religious movements. Between 1900 and 1930 approximately 2,250,000 Blacks left the rural south; most emigrated to large northern cities.[2] This growth represented an increase of over 400 percent in the Black population of the north; in Detroit, the increase exceeded 611 percent.[3]

The industrialized north had been viewed by many as a land of abundance, holding the promise of a better standard of living, employment, and equality. Most Blacks however, suffered severe economic hardship during this period. Their sense of deprivation was intensified by the difficulty of adjusting to a new environment and inequalities they endured in the social realm. Economic pressure often moves individuals to focus on their religious faith with greater urgency, and in the ghettos this tendency not surprisingly took on political overtones. Blacks were beginning to emerge from the shadows of slavery, and their religion had, of necessity, always served a variety of functions. Indeed, Fauset hypothesized that Black Americans' traditionally high religious participation was in part the result of the lack of other channels open to them.[4]

C. E. Lincoln's research suggests that religious movements provided Black Americans the opportunity to participate in an atmosphere free from embarrassment or apology, these were places where they may experiment in activities such as business, politics, social reform, and social expression.[5]
As well, he maintained that participation was often motivated by a racial or nationalistic urge.[6]

The absolute and relative deprivation suffered by Blacks during the Depression would have exaggerated these tendencies on a large scale. The first groups to crystallize out of this initial ferment were the Moorish Science Temple, led by Noble Drew Ali, and the Universal Negro Improvement Association (U.N.I.A.) of Marcus Garvey.

THE TRUE HISTORY OF MASTER FARD MUHAMMAD

The Moorish Science Temple originated in 1913. Its leader, Noble Drew Ali, preached a doctrine that included a strict moral code and linked religion to nationality:

Christianity 's for the European (paleface) Moslemism is for the Asiatic (Olive-skinned). When each group has its own peculiar religion, there will be peace on earth.[7]

Salvation depended upon accepting a new nationality; followers became Moors. Although its central tenets were undeniably political, the group did not take political action. They stressed obedience and loyalty to the American flag, believed divine intervention would bring about the end of white rule, and therefore cultivated a political, peaceful adherence to the status quo.[8] The primarily religious Moorish Science Temple did, however, initiate overt political statements on the part of Black religion, and as many writers, Black as well as White, are continually keeping alive, "laid the foundation" for the movements that followed it. Noble Drew Ali's death saw the Temple virtually disappear; in its place, a more political group emerged. Bear in mind that for an organization to have existed with various aspects identical does not mean that either was purposely design to serve as a spring board for similar organizations that followed.

The Universal Negro Improvement Association originated in 1916 and was perhaps the most popular "back to Africa" movement in American history. The Garveyites, as they were known, invested their money and energy into amassing a large commercial empire, the goal of which was to see Africa become the homeland of all Blacks.[9] Like the Nation of Islam, the U.N.I.A. stressed Black independence through self-sufficiency. Indeed, Marcus Garvey himself originated the phrase "Up you mighty race, you can accomplish what you will,"[10] a rallying cry frequently used by the Muslims' Messenger Elijah Muhammad. The movement progressed to the point of electing a Liberian government-in-exile, even having its own representative to the League of Nations, but began to lose momentum when the President of Liberia understandably refused the U.N.I.A. entry to his country.[11] Marcus Garvey was exiled in 1927 and his movement then faded from prominence.[12]

No doubt, that a shallow exercise in study will reveal that when you study any discipline from a comparative stand point, varying elements of the disciplines will have similar traits; however, to suggest that one is parented by the other or that one is the legacy of another, is to miss any possible margin of differentiation. What would set them apart is the basis or objective for which each were created or established. Out of a vacuum, anything can develop; yet, one thing is certain: When an entity is spurned, intelligence dictates that to really ascertain the true essence of it, one must focus on at least three things: The objectives of the entity, the time line associated with it, and its achieved accomplishments toward its objectives. One could argue if whether or not Nobel Drew Ali and the Moorish Science Movement accomplished their objectives within the three years prior to the Garvey movement? One could equally argue the same when it comes to Marcus Garvey and the U.N.I.A.

There appears to be a great inclination for new writers, journalists and researchers to draw from the work of previous writers, especially when it comes to the early days of the Nation of Islam, because cameras, reporters and media interviews were elements which were not as welcomed then as they are today; consequently, most of the lies, fabrications, theories and the like, had been manufactured in part by "Negro journalists" working for white media. In those days, to be the "only colored" journalist automatically meant that you had to be the one who went and got the story about "colored" people and it had to sell or that journalist wouldn't eat; consequently, when it came to the Nation, a group that wasn't always in the media's camera (especially Elijah Muhammad), access to the Nation was difficult; so, if you could get access to "them" or get an interview, you were almost guaranteed a grub steak. What suffered were the facts and since lies, fabrications and the like sold, that's what white media bought. They didn't want the truth, because they were trying to discredit Elijah Muhammad and the Nation of Islam for all intents and purposes anyway. The same bad information is still perpetuated to this very day.

Wallace D. Fard, later interpreted by members of his movement as Allah. Or the Great Mahdi incarnate, first appeared in Detroit in July of 1930. Little is known of his early life and his founding of the Nation of Islam; the information that does exist is vague and often contradictory. Complementary myths concerning Fard's ethnic origins are diverse.[13]

Despite the writers' conclusion that information regarding the origin of the Nation of Islam's "founder," and/or his early life is often vague and contradictory, it doesn't stop them from raising their ignorance to the level of "knowing."

A case in point: In what many perpetuators of what's passed off as a classic work on the Nation of Islam,

C.E. Lincoln notes...

"...that among them is "a legend" that describes Fard as a black Jamaican whose father was a Syrian Moslem, and one that reports he was a Palestinian with a long history of participating in racial agitation."[14]

In terms of the role Fard was eventually to play in the Nation's theology, according to Hatim A. Sahib.[15]

"...two "myths" stand out. To Elijah Muhammad (later the leader of the Movement), he declared himself a member of the royal dynasty of the Hashimide Sheriffs of Mecca, while to Elijah's wife, Clara, he apparently stated he was a member of the tribe of Koreish (the prophet Mohammed's tribe)."[16]

The variations and contradictions are just as interesting if not saddening when reading "new" writings about a subject which has been raked over the coals so long, even a fool can tell that the majority of the writers just don't know and are "too educated" to admit it.

Morroe Berger writes,

"One of Drew's followers, according to 'some historians' of the movement, was a man known by the name of W.D. Fard or by several variants of it. Although Mr. Elijah Muhammad has told me that Fard never was associated with Drew, Fard did create his own sect, the Nation of Islam, or the Temple of Islam, from which the present "Black Muslims" directly spring....It was claimed that Fard was born into the Koreish, the tribe of Muhammad himself."[17]

THE TRUE HISTORY OF MASTER FARD MUHAMMAD

An interview, At His Home
Elijah Muhammad , 1965:

"I have read, Mr. Fard Himself, was He a member of Nobel Drew Ali's movement?

EM: No. He was no member.

Or was He a follower or something?

EM: He's independent; He's not a follower of any of them, He's not.

Was He associated in any way with Nobel Drew Ali?

EM: No.

These reports then, so far as you are concerned, are incorrect?

EM: That right, He was no follower of Nobel Drew Ali; He's no follower of anyone. He's self independent. He's self independent. There's nobody for Him to follow.

There's a book call, They Seek A City, written by Arna Bontemps and Jack Conroy, which stated it could be the case, and I just wanted to know from you what your thought of it?

EM: The writer didn't have an understanding, as with so many still writing; they don't have a good knowledge of what they write on the subject, but they want to hurry out with something. Have you read Mr. Essien Udom's book?

EM: I've read enough of that.

What was your impression?

EM: We have some good in there, but I could easily classify him with the hasty writers. He's too hasty in what he wants to write, and probably would write correctly, but he wants to hurry and get [his work] on the market. [Also] Eric Lincoln, they both have very good things in their work, but show undeveloped knowledge of just what's what...[18]

END INTERVIEW

Elijah Muhammad, Messenger of Allah, had permitted countless interviews, such as the previous one, to many journalists, and the majority of them, especially first time interviewers, almost always would ask about Master Fard Muhammad and His whereabouts; yet, it seems that there is a great appetite to settle with outside conjecture rather than what Elijah Muhammad tells them. The motivations vary depending on the person and the journalist's employer. What's so strange is that many of those who have been granted rare interviews are in fact the very ones perpetuating varying and opposite views of what they have received directly from Elijah Muhammad himself.

When you get at the root of all the opposition and make it bear witness to the truth of the Messenger, you have forced all the branches to do the same. For example, every Black opposer of Elijah Muhammad gets his or her idea of opposition from the whiteman of America. Now the white man has already borne witness to the truth, even though this is against his nature. Where does this leave his Black followers? Their ignorance makes them unqualified; yet, many of the opponents understand Elijah Muhammad's teachings, but for varying reasons, seek to mislead others. There are many Black writers who will admit the profundity of Elijah Muhammad's writings, which in actuality are directly from Master Fard Muhammad; still, they speak and write as though there is no greater knowledge beyond what they have gained, or are studying, that either comes from whites or distant sages from outside the country. They will even go so far as to seek out esoteric, mystical and theosophical systems, along with the respective sages of these bodies of knowledge, in a futile attempt of refuting Elijah Muhammad, which is the same as refuting Master Fard Muhammad.

Many attempt to pass their ignorance off as higher knowledge. Hakim Shabazz refers to Master Fard Muhammad as an Enigma,[19] which means that which is puzzling, inexplicable or incapable of being explained or interpreted; so, despite the blatant acknowledgment of uncertainty, like many other writers, he ventures out to "explain" - in his own words - the unexplainable. To assist him in the impossible, he seeks the aid of another Black writer, Charles E. Marsh, who is author of From Black Muslims To Muslims: The Transition from Separatism To Islam. Just the title of his book, alone, strongly suggests that at one time the Nation of Islam wasn't Islamic, but separatist. This helps clue us in on his intent to rationalize his idea by raking and scraping any tid bits of theory, inferences, or conjecture to prop up his conclusion, instead of permitting the evidence to dictate a conclusion.

Most of the Arab world, as well as whites in America, have used the false argument that the Nation of Islam are not "real Muslims." That they are not worshipping the "true Allah," that they have a manufactured version; therefore, when characterizing them, the buzz-word "Black" is put before the word Muslim to signal this perpetuation. Thus, the title "From Black Muslim to Muslim." This as well is consistent with the overall 1975 transition from the way Elijah Muhammad taught and administrated the Nation of Islam, and the way his son, Wallace Muhammad, eventually steered the Nation.

Wallace Muhammad didn't believe that Master Fard Muhammad was Allah (God), which was contrary to Who Elijah Muhammad had said, believed and taught that He was. Thus, after 1975, and the bloodless coup (overthrow) of the Nation of Islam, the "political evolutionaries" went to work siccing attack dogs and the like to explain the "new" Nation of Islam. From this same vein came books which beard the same hypocrisy fathered by Wallace. This frame of mind is evident in the title: From Black Muslim to Muslim.

As previously mentioned, a very sly and deceptive alternative to directly refuting who Master Fard Muhammad was, was to subordinate and downplay the profundity of what He taught by putting Him either in the same category with contemporaries or developing theories to establish the notion that the Nation of Islam had antecedents: An occurrence or event proceeding another or the conditional member of a hypothetical proposition.

When looking for antecedents, no attempt seems to be as difficult to prove, yet advanced so much as that of trying to show that the Nation of Islam was a direct result of Noble Drew Ali and Marcus Garvey's movements. There is some evidence that all three had similarities when it came to the people for whom the movements served; however, are these similarities significant enough to serve as grounds for saying they are forerunners of each other? Emphatically NO!

Of course, this subject could be developed point by point to substantiate the overall point; however, it is very possible and judicious to adequately examine the foundation or contents of "the wash" which would relieve us of wasting so much time waiting until it comes out in the rinse.

Noble Drew Ali, founder of the Moorish American Science Temple (1913) acknowledges Garvey's influence on his movement. His book, The Holy Koran-Seven, is replete with the teachings of Garvey.[20]

In these modern days there came a forerunner, who was divinely prepared by the great God-Allah and his name is Marcus Garvey...[21]

The author came to this conclusion with a mere, single direct quote, in his 42 page book; yet, to tie the Nation of Islam and Elijah Muhammad into this proposition he writes,

"It has been suggested that Elijah Muhammad was an active member on the U.N.I.A. (as well as the Ahmadiyya Movement. We should also note that Elijah emphasized the writings of Maulana Muhammad Ali, the eminent Ahmadiyya scholar)."[22]

Not only does Shabazz give no references regarding a so-called membership, other than a "suggestion," but he doesn't even tell you where the suggestion came from. One would get more than that from the grape-vine! He further seeks to rescue this conjecture by heaping on more conjecture by trying to associate Elijah Muhammad with the translator of the Holy Qur'an.

When referring to the Holy Qur'an translation by Yusuf Ali as well as Maulana Muhammad Ali, Elijah Muhammad would compare various translations of various verses and the respective translator's commentaries. What's odd is that Shabazz didn't include Yusuf Ali, for Elijah Muhammad emphasized his writings too, since Shabazz deems comparing the footnotes in the two translations of the Holy Qur'ans as "emphasizing."[23] This is but another frail attempt at associating Elijah Muhammad with another group or person merely because their writings were comparatively analyzed. Interestingly enough, though, Elijah Muhammad, in referring to Maulana Muhammad Ali, he would do so for clarifying the fact that Muhammad Ali, founder of the Ahmadiyya Movement, wasn't who he claimed to be, such as the Mahdi.[24] Still in the defense of Master Fard Muhammad and His proper identity, Elijah Muhammad used these people to clarify the truth and not to use them as spring boards for his teachings.

Within the same paragraph of the above short and weak "premise" of his assertion, Shabazz summarizes,

"Both Noble Drew Ali and Elijah Muhammad were influenced by Marcus Moziah Garvey's nationalism and theology, they merely translated it into Islamic terms....[25]

How could Shabazz summarize when he never presented any facts or support for the summary? He did not point out one instance to support his assertion that Elijah Muhammad was "influenced by Garvey's nationalism and theology" to, "merely" as he so nonchalantly states, translate into Islamic terms.

THE TRUE HISTORY OF MASTER FARD MUHAMMAD

One writer builds his conjecture and theory atop the conjecture and theories of former writers for the purpose of "explaining" better than the previous writer, but one thing is overwhelmingly consistent, none of them have furnished any evidence to show that they factually know the origin of Master Fard Muhammad, nor have they produced any evidence to support their claim that either Master Fard Muhammad or Elijah Muhammad, His Messenger, were associated in any way to the Moorish Science Movement or the Universal Negro Improvement Association. The fact that they can't explain, reasonably interpret and, mind you, are still puzzled as to Master Fard Muhammad's origin, is grounds to invalidate any of their conclusions; for in the field of logic, if one's premises are incorrect and/or faulty, then any conclusion arrived at is invalid or moot, to say the least.

You should expect to see many other books surfacing with the same intent of trying to subordinate Master Fard Muhammad to a "common man." This was one of the tactics used by the disbelieving, hypocritical son of Elijah Muhammad, Wallace Muhammad. History has borne witness that he did convince a great many followers of Elijah Muhammad, which could account for the Great Hypocrisy manifesting since 1975. Even before this phenomena, there was a great attempt at trying to discredit Master Fard Muhammad and Elijah Muhammad by Malcolm X; however, he didn't get "his" thing off the ground, and as history has it, he didn't have a physical man-child to carry his seed into the future, which means his future has been terminated! Even if he had 1000 daughters, they will never produce a seed.

He does have one spiritual seed, you can recognize him by his work.

There are still other books, pamphlets and newspapers perpetuating the same incorrectness, and being passed off as the legacy of Elijah Muhammad and the Nation of Islam.

It is the epitome of ignorance to deny the truth of a matter and at the same time admit that you don't have the facts. It is the height of folly when attempting to build an unsupported argument the size of a planet, then make an attempt at fitting it through a pin hole of speculation, theory, and conjecture. There should be a law against elevating such ignorance to the level of scholarship.

One of the greatest published attempts at discrediting the Nation of Islam was initiated by Simeon Booker and Ed Montgomery. Mr. Booker had written a book published in 1964, titled "Black Man's America;" wherein he stated that the Nation of Islam was founded by a "flimflam artist who served a 3-year sentence in San Quentin prison for a narcotics law violation." This aspect is mentioned because the same lies, but more extensive, were published in the San Francisco Examiner in 1963. In response to this poisonous venom which this snake, and those who helped him, spewed up about Master Fard Muhammad (Who in fact is Allah in Person and Who is the One and Only teacher of Elijah Muhammad), the Messenger publicly announced in response to the following article and challenge:

Muhammad Speaks

Dedicated to Freedom, Justice and Equality for the so-called Negro. The Earth Belongs to Allah

Vol. 2—No. 24   AUGUST 16, 1963   111   15c—OUTSIDE ILLINOIS 20c

Nation Of Islam Offers Hearst

$100,000

To Prove Charge

Beware of Phony Claims

By Elijah Muhammad

I, Elijah Muhammad, Messenger of Allah, told the Los Angeles "Herald-Examiner" Office on Monday, July 29, 1963, that my followers and I will pay the Los Angeles "Herald - Examiner" Newspaper $100,000.00 (one hundred thousand dollars) to prove the headline charge ("BLACK MUSLIM FOUNDER EXPOSED AS A WHITE") made against us; that we are following one Wallace Dodd with many aliases including the name, Fard; that he is the man that I am representing to my people as being Master Fard Muhammad (Allah in Person) who appeared among us in Detroit, Michigan, in 1931 and is the same person (Wallace Dodd).

The Los Angeles "Herald-Examiner" also printed his prison history in San Quentin Federal Penitentiary on a charge of peddling dope, and that he admitted he was teaching us

If he (Dodd) was teaching for money in those panic days in Detroit, he did not get it from us. Mr. Dodd, undoubtedly, must have been teaching the white people if he received any money at all, because we did not have any

WE DID NOT pay Mr. Fard any money to teach us and there are many who will verify this statement who are yet alive. We could hardly pay the rent of a hall in those days.

Sometimes they (the Be-

(Continued on page 3)

The Phony

The Savior

At left is the dug-up convict, Wallace Dodd, alleged by the sensation-seeking and anti-Negro white Hearst newspaper to be founder of the Nation of Islam in North America. At right, however, is the real and rightful Master Farad, of Mecca, who gave all to black people in America before returning to Mecca. The Honorable Elijah Muhammad has not only offered to confront the phony imposter invented by the Hearst press, but has exposed the deceit and has offered to pay $100,000 if they can prove their fraudulent claims. (See Mr. Muhammad's Column)

"I, Elijah Muhammad, Messenger of Allah, told the Los Angeles "Herald-Examiner" Office on Monday, July 29, 1963, that my followers and I will pay the Los Angeles "Herald - Examiner" Newspaper $l00,000.00 (one hundred, thousand dollars) to prove the headline charge ("BLACK MUSLIM FOUNDER EXPOSED AS A WHITE") made against us; that we are following one Wallace Dodd with many aliases including the name, Fard; that he Is the man that I am representing to my people as being Master Fard Muhammad (Allah In Person) who appeared among us in Detroit, Michigan, in 1931 and is the same person (Wallace Dodd).

"The Los Angeles "Herald Examiner" also printed his prison history in San Quentin Federal Penitentiary on a charge of peddling dope and that he admitted he was teaching us.

"If he (Dodd) was teaching for money in those panic days in Detroit, he did not get it from us. Mr. Dodd, undoubtedly, must have been teaching the white people if he received any money at all, because we did not have any.

"WE DID NOT pay Mr. Fard any money to teach us and there are many who will verify this statement who are yet alive. We could hardly pay the rent of a hall in those days.

"Sometimes they (the Believers) would give Him (Master Fard Muhammad) gifts such as topcoats, overcoats, ties, shirts, or a few packages of handkerchiefs-but money was so scarce in those days that we just did not have any. Just about everyone who believes was on the "Relief" In Detroit Including myself.

"I would like the Los Angeles "Herald - Examiner" to prove that this man (Dodd) was my teacher by bringing him to this country at our expense.

"Mr. Wallace Fard Muhammad, Whom Praises are due forever, the Finder and Life Giver to we, the Lost Found Members of that great Asiatic Black Nation from the Tribe of Shabazz, speaks 16 different languages. Can Mr. Wallace Dodd speak 16 different languages?

"Mr. Wallace Fard Muammad also writes 10 of the languages He speaks fluently. His native language Is Arabic (does Mr. Dodd speak Arabic?) of which we have in His handwriting and it is the best writing or penmanship In the Arab world.

"Let Mr. Dodd prove that he was among us; prove that he gave us our names. Let Mr. Dodd prove who was his secretary and where were the Identification cards printed, of which we have with us today and did he write the Arabic on them himself?

"If Mr. Dodd was The Mr. Wallace Fard Muhammad, why did not the F.B.I. arrest him for this teaching of truth? Let this paper prove these things before it headlines us as liars and worshippers of white devils.

"I would like to ask the Herald Examiner to give us a minute close-up or this fake (Mr. Dodd) who they would like to make the public believe is our Saviour. Even the description of this man's height and weight does not correspond to Master Fard Muhammad's, (to Whom Praises are due forever)

measurements. I know His height, His weight, the size of clothes and shoes.

"WHEN MASTER Fard Muhammad left us, it was in 1934. Again, let Mr. Dodd prove that he and I were together and that the Lessons that I am teaching to my followers are from him, and where were they given to me and did he ever examine me on what he gave me, and where?

"There are many questions that I could ask this Mr. Dodd about, that would prove to the world that this man is a fake that the Los Angeles "Herald-Examiner" has published. We believe this by the reasoning of such unfounded truth.

"Let the Herald-Examiner Newspaper put us in contact with this Mr. Wallace Dodd.

"We will show the world that the entire statement is false; that this Mr. Wallace Dodd is not Master Fard Muhammad, To Whom Praises are due forever.

"I HAVE warned you against allowing the devils to trick you into believing their false propaganda which they are spreading all over the world and especially among the so-called Negroes who have been the perfect model-slaves for 400 years and yet do not have freedom, justice, and equality from the slave-masters.

"And now these smart, scientific tricksters are trying to prevent them from enjoying a permanent salvation that Allah (God), under the name of Master Fard Muhammad to Whom all Praises are due, has offered us.

THE TRUE HISTORY OF MASTER FARD MUHAMMAD

"We who believe in Him are a living proof of this offer that we are now being blessed with, even though we are afflicted with persecution and death.

"You have those whom the Prophets prophesied of in Washington and in Rome (The Catholics) to deceive the whole world and especially the so-called Negroes. Look In your poison book, the Bible, Revelation 12:9- 13:4, 8, 14- 14:11- 20:10 and 21:8."

The Authority To Be An Authority

For a good tree bringeth not forth corrupt fruit; neither doth a corrupt tree bring forth good fruit. For every tree is known by his own fruit. For of thorns men do not gather figs, nor of a bramble bush gather they grapes. {Luke 6:43-44}

If I do not the works of my Father, believe me not. But if I do, though ye believe not me, believe the works: that ye may know, and believe, that the Father [is] in me, and I in him. (John 10:37-38)

The above verses are excellent choices when laying a base and setting the tone for what I am attempting to illustrate here. So many have and are presently trying their hands at defining, characterizing, labeling and explaining the origin of Master Fard Muhammad as well as who He is.

I, as well as the readers, must bear witness to the fact that if all of the aforementioned writers are using terms to describe their own assessment of the origins of Master Fard Muhammad with adjectives like enigmatic, obscure, baffling, puzzling, and mysterious, then the question must rise as to who actually KNOWS! In mathematics we are taught that to understand the unknown, we must calculate on that which is known.

The above verses from the chapter of Luke recounts the words of Jesus wherein he says that "For a good tree bringeth not forth corrupt fruit; neither doth a corrupt tree bring forth good fruit." The tree here represents something that is well rooted which serves as a producer or originator and that which something else comes from; the fruit represents the product. The product of the tree has no choice as to what it is; for it is only a reflection or product of the tree.

Jesus illustrates with the above simile a relationship which is universal, meaning that in nature, new life is only a reproduction of the life before it. All to say that a good tree can only bring forth good fruit and a corrupt tree will always bring forth corrupt fruit. This principle is so consistent that Jesus goes on to say in the second verse, "For every tree is known by his own fruit. For of thorns men do not gather figs, nor of a bramble bush gather they grapes." As this is so in nature and on the mundane or ordinary, earthly level, so it is on the spiritual level.

As the term "tree" is used to illustrate the origin of a fruit, the term "Father" is used the same; however, within the fruit lies a seed which can reproduce the tree, but not the fruit, because fruit comes from trees. We can't get fruit directly from seeds in most cases, there must be another stage such as a tree or vine.

In this case Jesus is referring to my "Father" in the same breath, in which he referred previously to the "tree." Like the tree, the "Father," is the origin of offspring sometimes called fruit. Only in this case, it is works which distinguishes from what "Father" or "tree" a product or offspring is from. Therefore, when Jesus said, "If I do not the works of my Father, believe me not." Why? It is because works, in this case, was the yard stick by which Jesus used to measure himself, with respect to the works the "Father" did. His intent was to show that he either represented the Father or/and what the Father did is what he wanted to be measured by.

Consequently, it was through this means of measurement which Jesus instructs that,"...if I do, though ye believe not me, believe the works: that ye may know, and believe, that the Father [is] in me, and I in him." Thus, one would have to know something about the tree or the Father in order to adequately measure Jesus or the fruit. This is where a reasonable degree of knowledge about nature and the scripture is absolutely critical and mandatory; whereas, to not possess this knowledge is to stand completely unqualified to speak one way or the other.

It was said that knowledge differs according to the capacity for it, according to the latent powers in a man. Hence there is a variety of stages amongst Prophets and others. Further progress is possible even beyond these stages, for divine knowledge knows no bounds. The highest stage is reached by one to whom all truths and realities are revealed untaught (not taught through scientist of this world's universities). This helps to explain why many of the writers who have attempted to explain Master Fard Muhammad have failed. As the Jesus said, "Ye are from beneath; I am from above: ye are of this world; I am not of this world." (John 8:23)

Is this not what Elijah Muhammad has been saying since he had come to public view and analysis? The real disposition, integrity and validity of this position is known only to him who enjoys it. We verify it by what some call faith, and by what is sometimes defined as reliance based on verifiable history.

THE TRUE HISTORY OF MASTER FARD MUHAMMAD

I don't want the reader to misinterpret faith in this scenario with "belief." For it is so easy to associate terms with our relative or current usage, but I want to relieve the reader of too much personalization with these terms; therefore, permit me to define what I means as I go.

Belief means to assent, to agree or to concur. Sometimes we will go along with a point, grant a point or give in to it or acquiesce. Why is it necessary to deal with this definition? I am trying to illustrate a point here and that is for one to "just go along," then that's all it is or to "just to submit" doesn't mean you are convicted; one may just go along for an immediate benefit or favor. We're still talking about "mere belief." If I told you there is a 747 jumbo jet in your closet, you could exercise your choice to "believe" me, regardless of the motivation, you can just believe if you wanted to - right! But what is it that makes us not want to believe that; what is it that inclines us to reject that?

Is it not so that our normal thought patterns produce certain probabilities which makes us prone to reject the fact that there is a jumbo jet in our closet? Whereas, in our minds, we speedily weigh, analyze and deduct any probability, and even if we don't absolutely reject it, our general response will be rejection. In our minds we have calculated the approximate size of a jumbo jet and the size of our closet and determine that such wouldn't fit, then we submit our finding as a rejection. So, the question once again is what is the name of the process which we have just exercised?

There is a certain type of calculating which we as humans have come to rely upon, and it is that reliance which makes us different from the animals of the field. We operate off projections of consistencies; we depend on things being constant or the same. Whereas, if your closet is still the same size as it was the last time you saw it, and if jumbo jets are generally still the same size, then your probability of it being to big to fit will still be valid, which means your thinking is based on those constants. It is this type of tabulations and calculations which permit us to refer to ourselves as being stable. Can you imagine what we'd be like if our environment changed without us being aware. We'd be stone crazy.

When belief is taken to another level wherein the element of reliance and confidence is brought into play, then we generally refer to that level of belief as faith. Does faith have a definition or is it just synonymous with belief?

When we talk about faith, we are dealing with a level of trust, confidence, reliance or dependence. Do we believe the earth is going to turn into the light of the sun tomorrow? I could have said: will the sun rise tomorrow, which isn't true, because the sun doesn't move; so will the earth turn into the light of the sun tomorrow? Most would say yes, which is not as important as why we believe that. Do we rely on that? Do we trust that this phenomena of the "sun rising" will take place? Do we have confidence that that's going to take place? Do we depend upon it being so? This is part of us understanding what faith is.

If I were to stick my hand in fire, would it burn? Suppose I told you that only happened in 1995 and as of 1996, hands don't burn in fire anymore? I probably could show you an example of a man walking across burning coals or a fire breather blowing fire out of his mouth in an effort to unravel your confidence that fire will burn hands, etc....

THE TRUE HISTORY OF MASTER FARD MUHAMMAD

What if I had paralysis, or deadness in my whole arm and put it into fire, would I get burned? YES, because regardless if whether or not I can feel it, the process of burning is still taking place. Why? Because as fire is still rapid oxidation and the hand or arm is still flesh, the reaction will still be materially the same, which we call burning! What am I getting at? You can rely or rest assured that as fire is still composed or made up of that which God created it to be, and when something comes in contact with it, the reaction will be the same. Why do we rely on the consistency of the process? Are we sure, and if so, on what basis does that surety rests? Being a believer is one thing, but being one of the faithful is a bit different. There is more of a trust, confidence and dependence factor involved. Please stick with me.

What makes us trust that the earth will turn into the light of the sun, or what makes us have confidence, or what makes us rely on that is its history of having done that for so long! Think about it. We have been experiencing this history at least since we have been on the planet-right! In fact, we take it for granted, so much so, that many of us have all but threw away any notion of wondering or thinking about it anymore.

Do we not take for granted that when we bite down in an orange that the vitamin C we have come to expect to be there will in fact be there? Not only do we take for granted that the vitamin C will be in the orange, but we take it another level in assuming that the vitamin C will nourish our bodies! Although we don't necessarily see it happening; we don't smell it happening; we don't taste it happening; nor do we feel it happening! If our liver decided that it wanted to protest and go on strike, you and I would be in serious trouble, but there is a supreme reliance on the Creator, Who created us as creatures, that if we put vegetation, fruits and grains in our bodies, these elements (foods) will nourish our organs and perpetuate our lives! This is faith based on verifiable history.

When we say we trust that our respective location will turn into the light of the sun tomorrow, that's faith; when we say that we trust that the air we breath through our mouths or nostril will furnish oxygen for our lungs, that's faith; when we assume that vitamin C is in an orange and it will nourish my organs, that's faith; and it is defined as history. Thus faith is reliance based on verifiable history. It happens over and over and over.

Many of us who draw our information from this world's schools, colleges and universities have been taught and have come to merely believe that history is those occurrences which have happened in the past. This is not entirely true. Sociology deals with following, analyzing and predicting patterns within a society. Now, when an overall platform is consistent, or a societal circumstance is predictable, modifications and manipulation can be injected to control results. These are the type of experiments that social scientists occupy themselves with.

An example of how this plays out is when the people are metered by their socio-economic-status. Where the family lives, what type of money the father makes and the type of schooling and training he has, are the determining factors, which western social scientists use to project what his children will do and be able to do for years to come; in fact, have done an interestingly thorough job. They have actually been able to set up a system based on economics, status and education, which are consistent markers to determine if one can "make it" in this society, for to be unqualified or lacking in any one of them, automatically means your offspring is doomed. You may have noticed that as far back as the early 1980's, students applying for college entrance and financial aid were asked questions like, "Are you the first one in your family to attend college?" This was for the real purpose of adjusting their system, although we were made to believe otherwise. What are we getting at?

If the social scientist of today can study the people, under a consistent system, and project what the people's offspring are going to be doing decades from now, what can men supremely qualified in the science of the universal laws of creation do? Is not the laws of creation more consistent that the so-called principles which Western World societies have been and are still based on? As we have been basing our lifestyles and confidence on their system, we may have forgotten about the universal system above, around and within us, a natural system which we have been taking for granted!

Is not the Holy Qur'an and Bible composed of projections which we call prophecies. Do not these books contain occurrences which are said to have happened and are predicted to happen? Did these books fall out of the sky or have there been human beings who have made these strikingly accurate projections?

Is it coincidental that all of the symbolism of both books is enveloped and clothed in natural elements or elements of nature ranging from the celestial bodies to the very insects under our feet and over our heads. The sun, moon, stars, goats, sheep, lion, bees, ants, trees, snakes, etc.... As this is so, we cannot separate these books and their content from the same creator and His laws and principles on which we have relied all of our lives, and that's regardless of who we are or where we live. All to say that for you to utter that you don't believe in the truths of either of these books would be to deny the very elements you have been relying on your whole existence and are still relying on for your existence. Some may be attempting to wiggle and squirm while you are wrestling with my premise, but as you breathe the breath to do so, you are still bearing witness despite yourself.

In one of 40 questions and answers which Master Fard Muhammad gave to Elijah Muhammad in a "second term examination," it reads, "Who wrote the Holy Qur'an or Bible? Will you tell us why does Islam renew her history every twenty-five thousand years?

Answer: The Holy Qur'an or Bible is made by the Original people, Who is Allah, the Supreme Being or Black Man of Asia. The Qur'an will expire in the year twenty-five thousand, nine thousand and eighty years from the date of this writing (from approximately 1934). The Nation of Islam is all wise and does everything right and exact. The Planet Earth, which is the home of Islam, is approximately twenty-five thousand miles in circumference, so the wise man of the East (Black Man) makes history or Qur'an to equal his home circumference: a year to every mile and thus, every time his history last twenty-five thousand years, he renews it for another twenty-five thousand years. What does this question and answer mean?

To begin with, the question tells us that someone physical wrote both books and that Islam has something to do with this. What is Islam? Islam is the total submission to the Will of the Creator. Why didn't I say Allah? When we understand comparative religions, we come to understand that within each, the "God" of the respective religion raised up or sent His representative for the respective work among that given people; whereas, that prophet or messenger had to relate God's message in the language of the people to whom he was sent; therefore, he would call God's name according to what the people's language was; thus, the different names of God: Elohim, Yahweh, Jehovah, etc.... Yet, as both books prophesy, in the "last days," we would see God as He really is. Why? Because before Elijah Muhammad, none of the messengers had seen God, which is why the peoples of the earth thought God was a spirit.

According to the aforesaid prophesy, when God manifested Himself in the "last days," He came in a form in order for the people to see Him as He is."[26] But, what I am driving at is that in the last days, God would have a name that would include all the names by which He has been represented and that name is Allah, which simply means the All In All. So when one says the name Allah, they are simply saying all the names of God at once. Why is this so important? When the term Islam is used, we are simply talking about a state of being. Islam means peace and its significance means the making of peace; therefore, when the planets rotate in harmony, they derive a state of peace. When the elements in nature act in accord with each other, it produces a state of peace, because all elements are turning one way which is where the term universe comes from. Uni comes from Latin, which means one[27] and verse comes from Latin as well, which means vertere: to turn.[28] When put together, they mean to turn one direction or with oneness. The state produced as a result of turning in oneness is called peace in the English language and Islam in the Arabic language. So, when one compliments the consistencies of nature or the natural laws of the universe, one is actually bearing witness to the state produced, which is peace or Islam.

This state is renewed every twenty-five thousand years. As the answer goes on, it states that the two books, Qur'an or Bible is made by the original people, how? Similar to the way that the present day social scientists renew their programs to rule you and me. Their knowledge is limited, which is why their societies are corrupt and flawed, but the original Black people base their society and the ruling of their societies on the natural laws and principles governing our planet, which is why they can project according to the turning and circumference (the distance going around in a complete circle) of our planet. It is the consistency and reliance based on the planet never changing or deviating, which gives us confidence in making accurate calculations as to what can happen and what can't. If there is something we don't want to happen, we have wise scientists who can manipulate various elements in our universe to alter events for our best interest. This is why the prophesies in the books will take place, because the basis on which they rest is on the same system that you and I take for granted, but never has failed us yet. The natural laws of the universe are the foundation for the books, and the fathers of the Original Black people are the ones who wrote them - our Fathers. The circumference of our planet is 24, 896 miles. Approximately 25,000 miles. 24 scientist write our history. 23 do the writing and it is then brought to the 24th and He acts as Judge to determine what will come to pass and what won't. This 24th one is called Allah, the Supreme Being. Notice He is called the Supreme "Being," this is because He is human like you and I. The difference is that He is The Wisest Human. All of us have some wisdom and since we as black people are direct descendants or offspring of God, we are all Allah, it's just that there is One wiser than us all and this is what makes Him Supreme. How this will factor into Master Fard Muhammad's coming will be discussed in forthcoming chapters; however, my intent here is to show that the very books which the "critics" don't use in the "explaining" of Master Fard Muhammad, is the primary tool necessary for explaining!

This perspective is thus submitted in order to make this ultimate point. As we have demonstrated that the writers who sought to "explain" Master Fard Muhammad, Elijah Muhammad and The Nation of Islam are in fact unqualified to explain, because: 1) They manifested their own ignorance when it came to the origin of Master Fard Muhammad; therefore, any one coming in His name or using Him as the standard of measurement for their action, is beyond the comprehension of many previous writers; 2) The Messenger of Allah, Elijah Muhammad, said throughout his mission, which came strictly from Master Fard Muhammad, Who Elijah Muhammad said is God in Person and that the origin, aims and purpose of Allah (God), Master Fard Muhammad, is clearly in the scriptures, both Holy Qur'an and Bible; then if previous writers don't use the scriptures as their basis for explaining, defining or analyzing Master Fard Muhammad, then quite frankly, it's like using a chocolate cake recipe as a standard of measurement for a plumber; and 3) If they don't use the scriptures as the basis for determining if He is Who He says He is, or Who Elijah Muhammad says that Master Fard Muhammad or he himself is, then all their writings have been a supreme exercise in futility all the time!

As many have borne witness to the profound changes that have occurred as a direct result of Messenger Elijah Muhammad's works, the profound changes experienced by black people in America, and the unmatched affect he has demonstrated on the world, then one must bear witness to the fact that regardless of what others may have said about who Master Fard Muhammad is or isn't, no doubt that as Elijah has always said that his instruction came from Master Fard Muhammad, indeed Elijah Muhammad and his followers have most surely gotten the most benefit from his coming and presence, which stands to reason that Elijah Muhammad is the most qualified to explain who He Is!

"If I do not the works of my Father, believe me not. But if I do, though ye believe not me, believe the works: that ye may know, and believe, that the Father [is] in me, and I in him." (John 10:38)

My advice to the hasty, ill-informed writers, critics and hypocrites is to calculate on Elijah Muhammad's works when attempting to ascertain who it is that he represents. For you need to KNOW the Father of his work in order to KNOW if he did the work; for most surely if Noble Drew Ali or Marcus Garvey were his fathers, then surely, according to the words of Jesus, Elijah Muhammad would have done the same thing they did, and what Drew and Garvey had in common is that neither lasted too long; therefore, had he used what they used, he wouldn't have lasted as long as forty (40) years; likewise, even if you still don't want to accept what Elijah Muhammad said over forty (40) years, regarding the origin of Master Fard Muhammad, then there stands his irrefutable works still looking us in the face at this late date.

Perhaps if they would analyze it closer, without bias, they may come to believe the works which may help them come to KNOW and believe that which they have been puzzled about, unable to explain, incapable of properly interpreting and seeing darkly, and that is the Father of what Elijah Muhammad and the Nation is all about: Allah (God), Who Came in the person of Master Fard Muhammad.

I can not deny that the Honorable Elijah Muhammad admired both Noble Drew Ali and Marcus Garvey. Ali was the first Black man to make an attempt at bringing Islam to the Black man and woman in America and a great teacher was he. No one can deny the grand and noble work of Marcus Garvey; yet, the truth is, if you study the actual facts taught by the Honorable Elijah Muhammad, you don't see that in the writings of Marcus Garvey or in the writings of Nobel Drew Ali. Teachings like: What is the square miles of the Planet Earth? How much is the land? How much is the water? What are the exact square miles of the useful land that is used every day by the total population of the Planet Earth? What is the distance of the Sun to the Earth? What is the distance of Mercury to the Sun? What is the circumference of the Universe? What is the diameter of the Sun? What is the temperature of the Sun? Marcus Garvey and Nobel Ali didn't teach this!

The Bible said that when God came, He would measure the Earth and the water[29] and He would tell us what the earth weighed and what the measurement of the Earth is. Garvey and Ali didn't teach this; in fact, Sigmund Freud didn't teach this; Plato didn't teach it, prophet Muhammad of Arabia didn't teach it; the Holy Qur'an did not mention it and the Bible did not teach it. The Bible only said that when God came, He would give us the measurements of the Earth and the universe. Why? Because God knows the square miles, the inches. He knows how much water is in the oceans, plants, animals and atmosphere. So through Elijah Muhammad, He taught us the square mileage of the Earth: How much is land and how much is water. He taught us the square miles of the islands, planet and our universe.

It is not strange to scholars of Elijah Muhammad that white scholars had begun to approximate their figure in their encyclopedias and books of science to those figures taught by Elijah Muhammad, Messenger of Allah.

The question must be asked, how long has the white man been making progress? Look at his information explosion on his (information highway). Since when? When did white people learn how to crack and split atoms? Who taught it? Where did they get it. When did white people learn how to go into the genetic make-up of a thing, to correct things that needed correction? Elijah Muhammad was teaching this before they even found the magic bullet to challenge polio!

You see, we who are authentic, sincerely followers of Elijah Muhammad are not fools. Wisdom is known of it children. If we are wise, it is because of Elijah Muhammad only. We were not produced by Yale, USC, Princeton, Harvard or Howard!

It was from Elijah Muhammad, Messenger of Allah, who taught us how to use language and was actually given and English Lesson. This knowledge enables us to not only excite the imagination and stirs the consciousness of our people, but he taught us how to seed and feed the unconscious mind.

When Elijah Muhammad, Messenger of Allah, taught us of the weight of an atom and the fact that of how God created Himself, where in the writings of Garvey and Ali could that be found? When Elijah Muhammad, Messenger of Allah, taught us of the speed and the power of thought, where in the writings of Garvey or Ali did these men teach this? When Elijah Muhammad, Messenger of Allah, taught us of tuning in on another persons thinking, where in the writings of Garvey and Ali was this supreme science taught?

When Elijah Muhammad, Messenger of Allah taught us about the Earth and the moon, that the white man had to go to the moon to find out if it was true. But who sent him there? What gave him the thought that he could even go there?

When this white man was inspired to go into his laboratories to study the life germ under the telescope and advance to the stage of cutting out this or that from the chromosome that he didn't like, where did he get this knowledge from? He didn't get it out the Bible, nor did he read it from the Holy Qur'an. He got if from the teachings of Elijah Muhammad when he taught about their (white people's) origin. When Elijah Muhammad taught about their father, Yakub, they began to study it. Although they made the common man, as well as the ignorant Muslim, believe that it was a made-up fairy tale, they are now eliminating diseases in people before they are even born. All from the teachings of Elijah Muhammad. Now I ask once again, DID GARVEY OR ALI TEACH THIS?

Many called Elijah Muhammad's teaching fantastic, and far-fetched when he taught of the white race's father, Yakub. They called it foolishness when he taught of the white race's origin. Marcus Garvey and Noble Drew Ali didn't teach that; in fact, Moses didn't teach it, Jesus didn't teach it, prophet Muhammad didn't teach it, and there is not a scholar on the planet, black or white, who has come forward to make Elijah Muhammad, Messenger of Allah out of a liar!

When Elijah Muhammad asked the world: "WHO IS THE ORIGINAL MAN?" Marcus Garvey didn't asked that question! Nobel Drew Ali didn't ask that question! Jesus didn't ask that question! Moses didn't ask that question!

Where in the writings of Garvey and Ali can you find how the other planets were made? Where in the writings of Garvey and Ali can you find the science of microbes? Where in the writings of Garvey and Ali can you find the weight of the Earth? Where in their writings can you find why the moon is of the same materials of the Earth and the moon's affect on the life-blood of our nation? Where in their writings can you find the term Asiatic?

For those of afro-centric and nationalistic thought, you never heard of this term until Elijah Muhammad taught that the whole planet was called Asia and we were Asiatic Black people. You thought is was talking about another land mass where yellow and brown people lived. Surely if Garvey knew he was an original Asiatic Blackman, he would not have referred to himself and his organization as Negroes.

I could go on endlessly pointing out the shear fact that as great and noble both, Noble Drew Ali and Marcus Garvey are, it is easier putting a camel through the eye of a needle than to prove that Elijah Muhammad was a continuation of either of these men.

It is becoming very fashionable to promote that Elijah Muhammad had a legacy or knowledge passed down to him by Garvey and/or Ali, especially when attempting to give some kind of intellectual continuity to the Black Experience here in America. In a vain effort to shore up decade old theories and guesses about our identity and origin, many afro-centric and nationalistic theorists have found it very convenient; yet factually deficient, to link Elijah Muhammad with Garvey and Ali. They believe that by perpetuating that Elijah Muhammad merely had handed down teachings, it would in affect give legitimacy to their dead-in-the-water dinosaur schools of thought, take credit for the greatest work to have ever been witnessed on our planet and refute Elijah Muhammad's claim of being a Messenger of God simultaneously.

No one is attempting to take credit from Garvey and Ali. My attempt is to help set the record straight with facts. How the true followers of Elijah Muhammad feel about these untruths doesn't seem to bother the advocates; therefore, very little, if any, is reciprocated. There is no such thing of a legacy of Elijah Muhammad from Garvey or Ali. We must force those who advocate that Elijah Muhammad got his teachings passed down to him from Marcus Garvey and Noble Drew Ali to either prove it or be condemned as liars and enemies of God, His Messenger and the Believers!

Nasir Makr Hakim,
Minister of Elijah Muhammad,
Messenger of Allah

A Child Born In Heaven
Chapter 1

According to the Christian calendar, February 26, 1877, a Saviour was born for you and I. The Christians know about it. They know you think that what you're preaching happened two thousand years ago, but it is now taking place today. They know that, but they don't like you knowing it, because this is your salvation and their damnation. That's why they hate Elijah Muhammad, because they know Elijah Muhammad knows this truth that they have kept hidden from you. God has revealed it to Elijah Muhammad and Elijah Muhammad is telling you. He's teaching you. They dare not try disputing it. They will not come out in the open disputing with Elijah. They will take Elijah back in the jail, in the cell there and dispute with him, where you can't hear nothing. They won't dare come out here in the open. No., because they know Elijah knows them. They know Elijah has been taught the truth, the true knowledge of them and he has been taught the understanding of the Bible; therefore, they don't want to contend with Elijah in your presence. They want to contend with Elijah out of your presence. They have talked to me many times out of your presence, but they don't argue with me. They even agree with me. They go so far as to say it is time that your people know this, but they can't tell you. How can the same man who lied to you and have you going wrong, killing yourself - and many have been killed by that lie - come back and tell you: "I lied to you." No, you would be ready to kill that kind of fellow. That's right. He can't tell you, but he knows that God has given that knowledge to one of you. And its up to you to believe it or suffer the consequence!

The Bible says that Jesus was the son of God. If we understand the Bible, it also says Ephraim was the son of God and was the first born of God.[30] According to the Bible, even Ezekiel is given the title of the son of man.[31] He's referred to as the son of man. And according to the prophecy of Jesus in the Bible, he refers to a son of a man coming to usher in the judgment of the world and sit as judge.[32] This one is coming to sit as judge of the world, the son of man. He was not referring to himself, but a son of man. A man whom God will send at the end of the world's time, meaning the white man's world. A man will judge a man. We're getting some place now. We're getting knowledge now.

Let's see that baby born in heaven, that baby coming in the last days. Could we ever be made to believe that a man-child is going to save us? Since we believe, according to the teachings of the enemy, that God is a spirit. How can we ever be made to believe in flesh and blood as being a God? Let's piece it apart.

If God is a spirit and is not man, could we receive the son of man? Nevertheless, according to the Bible, God made man in the image of Himself and in His likeness.[33] Then could God be something other than a human being? If He's a spirit, he has no life. He's no image, if He's a spirit, because a spirit neither has a form at all, nor any likeness, nor any color. You can't give the spirit a form, but the spirit goes into a form. Is that right? Or rather, the base of a spirit is form.

Could you receive a son of man, representing himself as being the God in the last days? Could you do so? Since you have been taught that God is a spirit, you are greatly deceived. You would not receive a spirit representing himself as being God and you couldn't even see him. You would doubt it very much. Tonight, if you would lie down and go to sleep and you heard a voice in your sleep saying, I am God and I'm walking around here in this room, you could say that you dreamed that; yet, when you awakened, you wouldn't see that thing walking around in your room. Therefore, you still would doubt, because you want to see it. You would say, "If you say that you are God and you are walking around here in my room, what do you look like? Why don't you make yourself known to me?" All right. Now, that kind of God could never represent himself to us, because we're never going to believe the voice until we see where the voice is coming from. You're too intelligent to believe anything like that.

If a man comes to you, and you soon learn that that man has more wisdom, more understanding and is more powerful than you are, you will be inclined to start following him, because wisdom demands such. A superior knowledge demands submission from inferior knowledge. Now then, if a man in flesh and blood will come to us and he has more wisdom, knowledge and understanding than we have, and by his wisdom and by his understanding, he can do more than we can do, we will be forced to believe him and follow him. As it is written and I believe it, "Behold, the Son of Man cometh.[34] The Son of Man. I believe in the Son of Man, but I don't believe in no son of a spook. I don't believe spirits can produce me a son, but I do know a man and a woman can.

According to the Bible, in the Revelation, it prophesies that there is a wonder in heaven.[35] Let's see now where is this son coming from in the last day. "And I saw a great wonder in the

3

heaven, a woman clothed with the sun, and the moon under her feet and upon her head a crown of twelve stars." Who is that? "That's Jesus." Certainly it's Jesus, but not the Jesus of two thousand years ago.

If he said that he saw this woman clothed with the sun, and the moon at her feet, and have said that this was Jesus of two thousand years ago, how do you account for the twelve stars? "That was his disciples." All right, let's see then. You're right there. Then how do you account for the sun? How do you account for the moon? Then how do you account for the woman? "That was Mary." Well did Mary have twelve stars upon her head and a crown? What was she crowned for? Let's get down to business. This is something you should know.

A crown represents authority, a ruler. Stars represent justice.[36] We use them to justify a man when we pin a star on him. He's justified in having this degree of authority to go out there and arrest men. His authority is represented by a star, meaning justice. All praises due to Allah.

If God has prepared a woman in heaven, of whom is said to be a wonder, how could Mary be a wonder? If you say it's Mary, how could she be a wonder in heaven when her son said, "No one had ascended to heaven.?"[37] Are you saying that that was the spirit of Mary or a vision of Mary? This woman is in heaven, he says, yet, he didn't point out where the heaven was. He did not locate the heaven for us. Whether it was on earth or in the sky or off the earth. Is that right? This is the way we piece the thing apart so that we can get the understanding of it. If the woman has twelve stars on her head and she has a crown, and we know that in our own earthly government we represent men of authority by stars and by crowns, then if this is a wonder, there is something here we must learn. Why is it a wonder that the woman is in heaven? Do you mean to say that there has never been a woman in heaven? It couldn't be a wonder because of her merely being a woman in heaven, for other women were probably once in heaven or is in heaven. "And she's clothed with the sun." You couldn't imagine a woman sitting in the hot sun. You couldn't imagine a woman having the moon at her feet, a great big moon near half as large as the earth, but if they had said that the woman's feet were upon the earth, it looks simple. They said, she has the moon at her feet and she's sitting in the sun or she's clothed with the sun. Doubtless that everyone of us is clothed with the sun. We all lived in the sun. Is that right? And we all are clothed with the sun, but what does this particular book mean by that? We're going after that baby who is born.

According to the prophesy, it says that by one man came sin.[38] By that man, death came, but by another one, life came. Well now, there is something you have not yet understood one hundred percent.

This woman, she's sitting in heaven and is a wonder. A great wonder. She's clothed with the sun, with stars upon her head. You couldn't imagine great big planet-like stars sitting upon anybody's head, but it means something. The average of our people, I have tested them, actually believe it as it reads there. That's the thing, I want to bring you into the knowledge of what you're reading. It is wrong to believe it like that.

Now, let us take a look at this. The woman, sitting in the sun, she has a crown upon her head and twelve stars. Let's look back over here at what Joseph saw. Joseph, before he was put into authority, he saw the sun and the moon and he saw twelve

5

stars.[39] We see the sun and the moon and numerous stars. We can't count the stars that we see around the sun and moon, but Joseph saw the sun and the moon and twelve stars. And he saw eleven stars bowing to one star. And he saw the sun and the moon give way and bow to that one star.

Now these things must be understood. If we are having something similar to what we are discussing, we must break it all down. Joseph saw himself. He was the twelfth star. The book says, he was one of the twelve sons of Jacob. The book also says it meant that Jacob and his wife, which would represent the moon, would bow to their son, Joseph. All praises due to Allah. Let's have patience. His eleven brothers were going to bow to him as the ruler.

No where in the Bible does it teach us that Joseph was ever made King. All right then, if Joseph never did become King of a nation, then this vision he had could not mean Joseph alone, but rather Joseph himself, his family, and his brethren still represented something yet to come. All praises due to Allah. So the Surah (verse) said that 'he saw a great wonder in heaven,' a woman sitting clothed with the sun. According to the Bible, it says there is no necessity for the sun in heaven.[40] Heaven doesn't need the sun, nor the moon, according to the Bible. Well how then did the prophets see this woman sitting in heaven and sitting in the sun. We're only just chasing your belief, that's all.

What is it Elijah? Go ahead and tell us! I don't like to say so much, because I know you pretty well. You are a jealous people. If you can't be the first to say a thing, you disapprove of it or you don't want to believe it, because you didn't say it

6

first. I know you pretty well; I was born with you. I know you pretty well.

It means this my beloved brothers and sisters: The wonder, which this woman in heaven was, actually wasn't a woman of heaven. She originally was not a woman of heaven, but yet she's going to give birth to something of heaven to be sent out of heaven. All praises due to Allah. I hope you don't think I'm an infidel and I hope you don't disbelieve after truth comes to you. I don't want you to disbelieve. Truth is simple and it will surprise you when you know that simple truth.

Who is it that's talking about seeing a woman sitting in heaven? Who is that man? Do you say John the Revelator? Who is John the Revelator? It could not have been Jesus' disciple looking at his own birth after he had been born. I'm sorry preacher, you should shake hands with me if I'm telling the truth, which you did not understand, and let us all go together. Don't think hard of me. Thank Allah for revealing it to me so that you could learn it.

This woman that is sitting in heaven and is seen by someone, it was not a disciple of Jesus, two thousand years ago. You say, she's clothed with child. What are we to understand about that child looking like the sun. If that woman is pregnant with a child which the Surah (verse) says to you and I "its like the sun." What does it mean? How are we to understand such? This woman was not originally a member of the heavenly people. This woman was one that was not of the people of heaven, yet she is there to bear the child.

You, everyone of you that I see sitting here before me, you are people of heaven. You originally came from heaven, but this

7

THE TRUE HISTORY OF MASTER FARD MUHAMMAD

woman did not come from heaven. She was not even born in heaven. Her parents were not of the heavenly parents. Not that woman; yet, she's seen in heaven and is clothed with the sun. She's not the sun herself, but is clothed with the sun. She's not the stars herself, but she has them upon her head.

She didn't put the moon at her feet; yet the moon is at her feet, because she's clothed with the sun. The sun and the moon cannot be equal. The moon is always under the sun. All praises due to Allah.

This is a child that is being prepared in heaven[41] to be sent out of heaven to a people that had once been a member of the heavenly family. To bring that people back to heaven, he must have a body from a woman that is not of heaven, but of the people that he's going among to get that people who originally belonged to heaven. I hope you will have a little patience. I can't tell you this just so quickly.

You and I originally was of heaven and the white man brought us into this part of the earth and has made us like himself. He has made us practice and do the things that he does. "The only difference in us and the white man it is just the color.[42]" Now, since we have been born and reared up, taught, and schooled by the white man for four hundred years, it takes more than the common mother or the common son to go and separate these two people. It takes one powerful than either side. So, that one who is going to separate the two, he must be part of both. He must be part of both, I repeat! So that he can get next to both sides!

Here, the woman is seen a long time before she gives birth to such a child. She was seen six thousand years before the birth

8

of that child. She was seen among the Holy people carrying a child. Who's government was going to be like the sun. Carrying a child who's government or his teachings or his religion, as you would call it, would be as clear as the sun and that his truth, his government, his religion would block out or make the old religious world or the old religious teaching vanish, as the day sun blocks out the light of the moon. And the old world, or the old prophets' dispensation, they would become like the moon.

We have lived under the prophets' guidance for six thousand years. We have lived under the vision of prophets. God has revealed himself to prophets in visions and in dreams and we have followed them. But now, at the end of that time, here is a woman that's going to give birth to a child who's word and who's knowledge and wisdom is so superior to that revealed to prophets, that it will outshine their wisdom like the sun outshines the moon.

Are we going to live in the sun now? Jesus defines night and day. They're signs of the two worlds. The world of the enemy is kept with a little, small light so we may see our way to walk in the way of righteousness by the prophets. The Prophets' coming to the world of the wicked black stars are like a moon. They give a little light, because that world is a world of darkness. They prophesy and bear witness that a sun is going to rise one day. They are not needed. They are not necessary after the sun rises. Your moon, last night, was alright while it was night. The light looked beautiful, because we didn't see nothing else that was superior to her light.

The stars rose early in the morning just ahead of the sun, beautiful isn't it. Sometimes it looks like you almost ought to

9

see a shadow by it; nevertheless, it was only bearing witness that there is a greater light than I coming up after me. Hold your peace. We got to give birth to this child. After the duration of the night, there isn't anymore need of the moon or the stars, so we must now be living then in the day time: "and I saw a city where God Himself was the light,"[43] he said. And they need not the sun nor the moon, referring to the old world, referring to the prophets. And the Bible closes. The old Bible closes with the last of the prophets. No more prophets after Elijah, according to the Bible.

This baby, this woman, the woman there represents a woman and it also has another, a second meaning. It represents the people. Some of the theologians call it the church, but I also would bring you into a better understanding of it. It doesn't mean a Christian church as you understand it. It means a temple or it means rather the believers, that army of believers in the last day. And again, it means a Messenger or a prophet in the last day, who is always styled or typed as a woman, because as a woman gives birth to children, a prophet, by his mission or knowledge of God, gives spiritual birth to the people. Therefore he's styled as a woman, because one brings the child to birth physically and the other brings a spiritual birth to that child. That's the way to understand it and the proper way.

The woman that he saw is as I said, a woman that was out from the world. She was not a woman of heaven. She was a woman of the world, but was chosen by heaven out of the world, and was claimed from the world to bear a child to be sent back into the world to bring back to heaven that particular child that had gone astray and had lost himself in the world. That child is none other than you and I, who was once in the heavenly family belonging to the Holy people, but now have gotten ourselves lost in the Western Hemisphere among a strange people; a people that is an enemy to us, a people that is not our people, a people that is no friend of ours. They have caused us to get lost from our own people and from our own God and from our own religion, by teaching us a false religion and of a God that doesn't even exist, in the name of a good one that you have knowledge of.

He put that name, that good name, on something that is false, which will make you incline to it, since you are divine people. You will follow the name and at the same time will not be getting the value of the truth that the name actually belongs to. That's what the white man has did for the so-called American Negro and all Black people that follow him.

He uses the name Jesus, but you should be wise that the white man doesn't want to recognize no Black prophet, nor any Black angel, nor any God that is Black. He's got to be a white prophet. He's got to be a white angel. He's got to be a white God for him to recognize him. He has you following that particular color, white, and he's indirectly making you believe or think that when you go to heaven, you will be white like himself. That makes you always incline to that particular color and desire of being that color instead of your own original color. He has you like that. He said to you, 'Jesus taught this religion; this is Jesus' religion,' but they are very smart, if you would contend with him and say, "How do you make that to be Jesus' religion?" 'Well,' he says, 'uh, Christian means to be one with God. Don't you believe that the prophet is one with God?' Yes. 'Well that's the Christian we are talking about.' Well you're not that. 'I didn't say I was a good Christian.' He'll tell you that. 'But I'll say that Jesus was a Christian, because Christian means to be crystallized into one. He was one and one with his father. And the father was one and one with the son Jesus.'

You can not over take him, but we have over took him and now running him. If you chase him and say, 'Where is the heaven you're talking about up there?' He says, 'well all of us refer to the open space as heaven. Don't you read how the astronomers refer to the heavenly bodies, meaning the stars and the other planets.' He says, 'all the space is referred to up in the heaven.' Then you say, Well, what are you talking about man for? He say, 'We didn't mean that the man actually go up into space. Heaven, you know, means a place of rest, in peace with God and in the likeness of God and under his protection and a place where there is no wickedness going on. That could be any place.' That's what he will tell you. It would be any place wherever there is peace. You can't chase him so easy unless you are real smart. If he would get you on one point, if you didn't know all the points, you would let him go, but if he gets me on that point, he's yet got plenty more I'm going to chase him on. You see, I'm not going to let him go with that, since you know it to be a simple thing. 'Then why do you teach babies to believe something that is not' when you know that the baby is believing he's going up in the clouds or up in the sky some place after he dies, and you know he's not. Why don't you tell the baby that it's not what you're talking about. What is your answer for teaching that baby to grow up under you as his teacher, dumb to the knowledge of actually what you are teaching?

Then he will grin. He'll say, 'Well, I gave them the Bible.' Yes, but if you gave them the Bible and you know the interpretation of the Bible, the right interpretation, why didn't you give him that? Then he will say, 'Well, maybe I don't know all the interpretations of the Bible. Maybe you know it better than I.' He'll lie like that. Then, you tell him, I'll tell you the reason you don't do it, it is because you're just a lying devil. That's all.

There is no such thing of God producing a son, two thousand years ago for the Jews, to be the redemption Christ for the Jews or to restore the Jews back into the favor of God. No Sir. That never has happened and never will happen. God doesn't want the Jew and no other white people. He doesn't want them. It is you that God wants. And it is the white people who have deceived you concerning God. You are deceived about the knowledge of God. You don't even know God, and if you chase the white teacher, he'll tell you, 'no man ever never seen God.' Then you say, 'Well, you lying blue eyed devil, what God are you teaching me to believe in when no man has ever seen Him, and know nothing about Him?' Then he will say, 'Well, You feel God; you seek God through prayer.' Say yes, but how about that baby over there that's bowing down to that statute there? Or how about that one over there in India praying to a monkey, or praying to some hand-made carved piece of wood, or praying to the river there? What about that? You see he can be caught upward, don't worry about that, you can chase him and make him to admit he's lying.

They hate Elijah. They call Elijah every thing they can think of other than good behind his back, because Elijah has been given the truth and that truth is the salvation of the so-called Negro.

I'll tell you how to overtake it brothers and sisters. You watch all college students and university students. You don't find them believing to much in Christianity. Why? Because he's getting too intelligent and learned. He sees that there are some

13

mistakes made here somewhere. What does doctors, lawyers and educators look like sitting down listening to you preach to him that when you die, you are going up in heaven. You're going to wear long white robes and you're going to eat at the welcome table. What do they look like listening to you talk that kind of stuff to them? They're not going to sit there listening to that kind of stuff, because they already know. They have studied life. They already know that nothing like that happens after a man dies. They will walk out on you. Is that right?

The majority of the time that you see lots of doctors and educators sitting around in church is the time when they think that the pastor is going to give them a break. Yeah, that's right. Give them a break: making some of you his [the doctor's] patients. He and the pastor are friends and you are the merchandise. I'm sorry Reverend, you and the lawyer and the doctor, I'm sorry, but Elijah is trying to get rid of all that particular profession anyway. In that day, you won't need doctors and you won't need any lawyers. In that day you won't need a lot of preachers according to the Bible. It says that, "one will be a shepherd for you."[44] My beloved brothers and sisters, let's give birth to the baby and go home.

He must be part of you and part of your enemy. He must look like your enemy in order to get among your enemy and bring their power to a naught, and yet, be a part of you. He must be of you. His father must be your father. He must be one like you; in that way, as the father is of the Blackman, he belongs to the Blackman.

The woman that's seen sitting in the sun, in the light of truth and in the midst of the righteous, is a wonder to see sitting, because she is not of that particular family. But what happened? The God cleaned her up. He stripped her of the devil and made her fit to give birth to a child, a child He intended to use to go after his people and to redeem that people from her people. I know it's hard for you to believe other than the way you have been taught, but this is truth. I will face all the white scholars and I will prove to you before their face that this is the truth and force them to admit it.

That man that comes after you, He came from a Holy Place. The Bible gives you this: It says, that by sin, death came upon the people, due to that one man of sin. And from that man came a lie. He lied. He deceived the people concerning God. He made the people disobey God. Now here comes One that is absolutely of the light of truth. He was not born in the world of unrighteousness. He was born in the world of righteousness. This Man, He's absolutely clear; He's pure and He is to bring a pure nation back to Heaven.

The untrue, the unrighteous, cannot be a redeemer for the unrighteous. It takes a righteous person to redeem the unrighteous; therefore, you have here again, that in the first Adam all died and in the second Adam, all lived.[45] All praises due to Allah. There you have two men's birth: carnal men, and some people say earthly people. Some think the second Adam is the Jesus of two thousand years ago. Not so. No, not so.
If God made Adam from the dust of the earth or from the earth and not from the essence of the heavens, but from the earth, the dust of the earth, then he's not from the heaven. All praises due to Allah; then Adam, that Adam is a very low man. He's considered nothing. As the dust is considered nothing.

In another place it says he made him from clay.[46] Well, old poor red clay won't produce anything. If you get that Black

15

loom that is rich earth, it will produce great crops, but not that old poor red clay. You're wrong. Here is a red devil that has been produced. He's a poor wicked thing that has been brought out of that same earth where that black earth is at. As the red clay is the poor part of the black earth, the white race is the poor part of the Black nation. I hope you will have patience. I'm going to let you go now in a few minutes. Here comes the redemption for a man or for a people that has been lost among another people so long that they don't even know their own people. Because they have lost knowledge of self, they don't know the people that they are among. They go only by color. They say this is a white people and we are dark people or we are brown people or we are red people. They go only by color. They don't know either one.

One must come that knows the tricknology that the other one has played on the other, and teach the ignorant one the knowledge of himself and the tricks that have been played on him by his wise enemy. That One to come must be prepared outside of the enemy. He can't be prepared in the same area. He must be prepared in heaven, so that no sin will touch him, until he is absolutely of the age to go after that one of his own people that is now lost and submerged into sin. He must destroy that one that has destroyed his own people. When the enemy sees Him, he will think its one of his own kind. "Behold, he cometh without observation.[47] All praises due to Allah.

The old writers, one of them said, 'I saw him, I saw him coming.' Doing what? Treading the wine press alone by himself.'[48] That was not the Jesus two thousand years ago. He didn't tread the Jews down and crush their life blood out of them. This Man coming in the last day, He must tread the wicked down and crush them as a man treads grapes under his feet and crush the blood of the grapes out. He must crush men's blood out of them - the wicked blood of the people. He said, 'And why is your garment so red?' He said, 'I looked and I didn't find no one to help me, so I did it alone; therefore, I have crushed them in my anger and my garment is spotted or stained with their blood.' Meaning what? Meaning that, this one man is going to destroy a whole race of people. That's what it means.

That Man was born in the year 1877, in the Holy City. That's your heaven to which your Bible is referring. He was born in the Holy City, Mecca. His father went out of Mecca, got the woman from up in the hills of Asia and brought her [down] and cleaned her of her own evil. The evil tendencies of the woman, the very spirit of evil was taken from her. And she was made a perfect, Holy and a Righteous woman, though not by nature; yet, made righteous.

You have it again, that in the Bible concerning the promised child. Isaac was a promised child.[49] Not one that actually belonged to Jacob, but he's a promised child. So it is with the race, the Caucasian race. They are not original people, they are grafted people out of the original people.

Now to reclaim or redeem a people that the grafted people have eaten up or swallowed, we must take from the grafted people something of the graft [a part like them] and take from the original people, [a part of the original people] that of the original and combine the two together. We then will put the combined product back among the grafted people and the people who are not grafted. The people who are not grafted will be brought out by the combined product or the Man made

17

from both, introduced back among the grafted people. You do not belong to the white race; yet, you are swallowed up by the white race and cannot free yourself from them. You can't come out of them, not to save your life, not by your own power and effort.

You can't even unite. I've been calling you to unite for the last twenty five years [sixty three years, today, 1996] and for the last three days here in this house. I know you can't unite yourself. The God of unity must unite you, but I'm doing my part. I'm sent to call you to the unity of God, whose proper name is Allah. I have not the power to unite you. I can't do it. If the word of God won't unite you, I have not the power to force you into unity. The power is from himself, but he sends the word first. And the word makes a distinction and that which is good will unite and that which is not good, it will fall off. All praises due to Allah. I hope you understand. I call you to believe in Allah. I know you can't believe in Him a hundred percent unless He pleases that you believe in Him, but I represent Him and His name, that it might make a distinction between the good and the bad among you. That's all that I want to do.

Now the baby in heaven that is born in heaven. Not that baby that is born in the wilderness. Here you have two babies in the Bible, in that same prophecy. The woman gives birth to a child or born with a child in heaven, and then there's a woman running in the wilderness. In the wilderness, there's a woman, she has a young baby. She's got to protect her baby from beasts. All praises due to Allah, but that baby that is born in heaven needs no protection, because that baby is as the sun. All praises due to Allah. When that baby left heaven, that baby produced a baby in the wilderness, then that baby becomes a

18

woman in the wilderness. She's producing a baby; however, her baby is in danger of being destroyed by a beast.[50] All praises due to Allah. I want you to understand your book. It's beautiful, if you understand it. It's just like playing with rattlesnake poison if you don't understand it. I say my friend, this is the wilderness of your Bible, it's America. The beast that will destroy the child is none other than the white man. The woman fled in the wilderness where she had a place. Until what? Until the power of the beast has been broken. The Bible don't teach you that. It don't say the power of the beast, but she must flee from the beast for a time and time and a half time, until the power of the beast is broken. And then at that time, she will have her child walking.

His name shall be called Emmanuel. God is with us. It did not happen two thousand years ago. It's today. "And I saw written on his side, Kings of Kings, Lords of Lords and he had another name that no man knew but he himself."[51] That's a name out of the, rather it's not numbered in the one hundred attributes of God's names. Therefore, the scientist didn't know what his name was since it is not coming under none of these attributes that makes up God's names.

What is his name then Elijah that you're representing? He came to us in the name of Fard.[52] What is that? It's a name that is absolutely, (well, to make it clear to you) you're compelled to observe and do this in the prayer service of Islam. That morning prayer service, it's called Fard and that it is made absolutely binding upon you and I to say. Because in the last days, a man is coming by that name, and it is going to be binding upon you and I to bow down to that man or else. The Fard, it is said by the commentators, is a name that means Independent and a name that is absolutely made binding and compulsive. We are compelled to submit to. But nevertheless, it is not one of the ninety-nine attributes, yet this is an independent name outside of these one hundred. What and why you should choose such names? He is a God that is not associated with any other God. He's a God that the others before him have no, absolutely no association with him. Your God is one God. No associates has He. Your Lord is One Lord, meaning that He is not One that is associated with the Twelve major or the Twenty four elders. They all must bow to him.

The Twelve major Imams, as they are called in Islam or in the Arab language, they don't have this one's knowledge. This one has a superior knowledge and that the other Twelve minor or the Twenty four elders, as you find them in the last of the book here, casting down their crown to that One that is conquering the beast and is delivering a people from that beast. They bow down to that One and give praise and honor to him. As though they never knew him before. Read it for yourself.[53] They say, worthy is he. As though they never saw him before. Then they said that worthy is the lamb. The lamb looked as though he was slain from the foundation of the earth. He was in a bad looking condition, but worthy is he. Why? Because he was the only one that the God would give his secret to, called the Book that he held in His right hand or that which He held within Himself and would not reveal it to no one, but something that was out of heaven: The prophet or a messenger, because he would receive from God that which no other prophet ever was able to receive. He is the same that the elders called a lamb and he's the same that the Revelations called 'a baby being born in the midst of beasts.' That's the one. One that is taken from among you, and the God that comes to you is the one that's born in the heaven.

That God also is born of God. He's born of God and becomes God Himself and then He also gives birth to a messenger or prophet of His own, that is not chosen by the other righteous. He choose his own man. Then He makes the others to bow to His own man like the father of the Caucasian race did in the year 8,400 or in the 9,000th year of our calendar's history when He was producing the white race. He made his man and then made us to bow to him, so will God in the last days: make Him a man and a people out of no people and then make the others to bow down to Him. All praises due to Allah.

You are to go on top, not at the bottom, but on top. Well, how are you going to get on top? Don't look at the physical, or rather worldly wealth. Don't look at that. It's the wisdom that God will give you which is superior to the white race and your own people that is in Asia. He will be with you. He will guide you. He will teach you what he didn't teach them. In your Bible it says, 'And God Himself was among them.' Your Bible says that God said, 'I will be their God and they shall be my people and I will lead them into the light of truth and they shall know that I am the God and that these are my people.'[54]

It is you that God now is visiting. It is you that God now wants to put on top of the world. What is meant by going on top? As ruler. He has said to me that if you will accept Him and the religion of His and the prophets, which is Islam. Islam means entire submission to God and when you submit to God you enter into peace of God. That is the kind of religion which is referred to under the name Islam. It's not a religion, but the nature of God and the righteous. Today the God of heaven has been born for you and for me, the so-called American Negroes, who are hated by every civilized people of the earth and will not be accepted as their equal. Now the God who is Supreme

21

over all human beings and has more knowledge than all, has chosen you who has less knowledge than all, to make you wiser than them all and to put you in the authority to rule the others forever and forever.

In my conclusion, let us all remember that there is no such thing as a Jesus born for you two thousand years ago. But remember, that a Jesus was born for you in 1877, and He's working in the midst of you in North America, and is sending plagues after plagues upon America so that the government of America may know that today you are not no more a forsaken race of people, but now you have been chosen, and there is a God on your side to defend you if you will only look to that God.

The Coming of The Son of Man Chapter 2

"For as the lightning cometh out of the East, and shineth even unto the West, so shall also the coming of the Son of Man be."[55]

"And shall appear the sign of the Son of Man in Heaven; and then shall all the tribes of the earth mourn, and they shall see the Son of Man coming in the clouds of Heaven with power and great glory."[56]

The final battle between God and the devils will be decided in the skies. The devils see Him and His power in Heaven and Earth. The nations of the West are in great pain trying to form their defense. Now is a very serious time on our planet and it will continue to be until the powers of this world are destroyed. The hour of this world has arrived. How will the Son of man win the battle against this world's use of space weapons?

As we now realize Jesus' prophecy of a man (Son of Man) coming at the end of the white race's (Devil's or the Man of Sin's) time which was up in 1914,[57] makes it very clear as to what we should expect. It is a man, the son of another man, not a spirit, as we all are sons of men. On that day, a Son of Man will sit to judge men according to their works. Who is the Father of this Son, coming to judge the world? (I will tell you soon in this book). Is His father of flesh and blood, or is He a "spirit"? Where is this Son coming from? Prophet Jesus said: "He will come from the East," (Matthew 24:27) from the land and people of Islam, where all of the former prophets came from. Jesus compared His coming as "the lightning." Of course, lightning cannot be seen nor heard at a great distance.

"The actual light (the Truth) which "shineth out of the East and shineth even unto the West," is our day sun. But the Son of Man's coming is like both the lightning and our day sun. His work of the resurrection of the mentally dead so-called Negroes, and judgment between truth and falsehood, is compared with lightning on an instant. His swiftness in condemning the falsehood is like the sudden flash of lightening in a dark place (America is that dark place), where the darkness has blinded the people so that they cannot find the "right way" out. The sudden "flash of lightning" enables them to see that they are off from the "right path." They walk a few steps towards the "right way," but soon have to stop and wait for another bright flash. What they actually need is the light of the Sun (God in person), that they may clearly see their way. The lightning does more than flash a light. It is also destructive, striking whom Allah pleases of property and lives. The brightness of its flashes almost blinds the eyes.

So it is with the coming of the Son of Man, with the Truth, to cast it against falsehood that it breaks the head. Just a little hint of it makes the falsehood begin looking guilty and seeking cover from the brightness of the Truth. Sometimes lightning serves as a warning of an approaching storm. So does Allah (God) warns us by sending His messengers with Truth, before the approaching destruction of a people to whom chastisement is justly due. They come flashing the Truth in the midst of the spiritually darkened people. Those who love spiritual darkness will close their eyes to the flash of Truth, like lightning, from pointing out to them the "right way," thus blinding themselves from the knowledge of the approaching destruction of the storm of Allah (God), and are destroyed. "As the lightning cometh out of the East so shall the coming of the Son of Man be."

Let us reflect on this prophecy from the direction in which this Son shall come: "out of the East." If He is to come from the East to chastise or destroy that of the West, then He must be pleased with the East. The dominant religion of the East is Islam. The holy religious teachings of all the prophets, from Adam to Muhammad, was none other than Islam.[58] They all were of the East and came from that direction with the light of Truth and shone toward the old wicked darkness of the West. The West has ever closed its eyes and stopped up its ears against the Truth (Islam) and persecutes it, thus making it necessary for the coming of the Son of Man (the Great Mahdi) - God in person.

Being the end of the signs, in His person, He dispels falsehood with Truth as the sun dispels night on its rising from the East. Why should the tribes of the earth mourn because of the coming of the Son of Man, instead of rejoicing?

The non-Muslim world cannot win a war against the Son of Man (God in person), with outer space weapons or inner space. It does not matter, for He has power over everything-the forces of nature and even our brains. He turns them to thinking and doing that which pleases Him. The great waste of money to build your defense against Him or the third world war is useless. You don't need navies, ground forces, air forces or standing armies to fight the last war. What America Needs to win with is: freedom and equal justice to her slaves (the so-called Negroes). This injustice to her slaves is the real cause of this final war. Give them up to return to their own, or divide with them the country that you took from their people (the Red Indians) which they have helped you to build up and maintain with their sweat and blood for 400 years. They even give all their brain power to you. They help you kill anyone that you say is your enemy, even if it is their own brother or your own brother. What have you given them for their own labor and lives?

Is it just a job or labor for you? You hunt them and shoot them down like wild game; burn them; castrate them; they are counted as sheep for the slaughter, all who seek justice. You have continuously persecuted me and my poor followers for years. Both fathers and sons are sent to prison. Just because we believe in justice and teach our brethren the same, we are imprisoned from three to five years and forced to eat the poison and divinely prohibited flesh of the filthy swine in our food, to your joy.

You set your agents around and about our meeting places where we are trying to serve the God of our fathers, to frighten our poor, blind, deaf and dumb people away from hearing and believing in the truth. With 50 states, which equal approximately three million square miles; with billions of dollars in gold buried and rusting, which we helped to get for you, yet none is ours; not the tiniest nor the most worthless state of yours have you offered your loyal slaves. Nor even to one square mile for their 400 years of labor.

Shall you be the winner in a third world war? The God of Justice (the Son of Man, the Great Mahdi) shall be the winner.

He is on the side of the so-called Negroes, to free them from you, their killers. As it is written, "Shall the prey be taken from the mighty or the lawful captives delivered? But thus said the Lord, even the captives of the mighty shall be taken away and the prey of the terrible shall be delivered; for I will contend with him that contend with thee. I will feed them that oppress thee with their own flesh, and they shall be drunken with their own blood. As with sweet wine, and all flesh shall know that I the Lord am thy Saviour, and thy Redeemer." [59]

The Son of Man is that Man Who is given authorities and power by God to carry out His judgment upon the people. That's what the Son of Man does. And then it goes on also for the Mahdi being born out of His nation by a woman that is not of His nation. The man that produced the child, that she give birth to, was of us, Black man, and that he married her to get an unlike child so that He can send that child among our people and his people to produce rulers out of us; those of us who were lost among the unalike people. That man Who was made from among his people and the enemy was and is the God of the judgment and the God to destroy the unalike, to whom we have been attracted and have followed for the last 6,000 years. The unalike is the white people; they are unalike us, and we are not like them. They are not like us by nature. That's why they call him mankind, because he's just kind of like the real man, but he's not the real one.

A God who is able to fulfill His promise to us, [having] come and offered you that Flag on the right (sun, moon, & star), means that it is time now to rule your own, that's your own, and He has offered it to us. We have a song we sing that's beautiful, it goes like this: "Allah has given to us, our own, the Sun Moon and Star for a Flag." I don't think you will find the

27

white people running all over the earth with that on their head, because they know better. They don't have a part in it; they have time in it, but not part of the creation. When you ask the white man about his secret order called Masonry, he wants you to answer that you were not made in that, but you were born in that. That is true. We are born Muslims and cannot be accepted by saying that I was made a Muslim. We were created Muslims.

The parable of the fig tree that Jesus cursed,[60] was also a sign of this world. This world has never produced converts to the Will of Almighty God Allah. Never has any so-called American Negro been taught by white people to believe in Almighty God Allah and His true religion, Islam. Only in higher Freemasonry is there a little teachings at the top, mostly of this particular order that mentions the teachings of Almighty God Allah, but you have to pay a lot of money to become a 33rd degree Mason. You become an absolute victim, as Isaiah teaches you, that you buy that which does not bring you any gain. To buy that kind of teachings does not gain you the hereafter. We must have something that is pure. A Mason cannot be a good Mason unless he knows the Holy Qur'an and follows its teaching. This book is the only book that will make a true Mason. The Bible won't make you a true one. If you are a true Moslem friend, then alright, lets have it in the open and not in the secret.

We use to buy Masonry, trying to make friendship with Satan. We go and buy that Crescent put it on our coat, laughing and looking at him when he passes, in words to say to him, "See, I have the Crescent on me; you should take me for your brother." We gave him that after he has shown us that he could act like us from 35, 40 or 50 years. We let him wear our Crescent;

that's ours. The red and the Crescent over it, that's ours. He can take his mystery [American flag] for himself, but if he wears that [Flag of Islam], look at him again, he worked for that, he didn't get that so easy.

The American flag has blue, which is an untrue color; you have many stars there. It takes all of those stars to try to justify something. It shouldn't be done like that. We got one star, which justifies [us], which represents all the stars, it's ours. There are six stripes of red in the American flag, not a solid background of red, because the red represents freedom, and he doesn't give freedom - only to those who are able and wealthy. If you're able to buy it from him, he'll give you freedom.

My followers are wearing it on their heads, because now God is turning over to the slaves, Blackman, the Universe, and they are within their right to put it on their head, because it's theirs.

If you don't see the white mason wearing it but once a year, you wonder then, wow, why don't we wear it along with them once a year. No, we're the father of it. If the father is going to lay his emblem aside to go along with the non-owner, then the father is doing this either to make an acquaintance with him in his own country, or the father is just laying his down for a certain time.

Today we are able to wear our fez which represents the universe, but white people don't do this, they wear them once a year in some kind of turnout, because this is not his, that's why he don't wear it. He's a man put in the universe for a time, and at the end of that time, he gets out of our house. If he don't get out, we throw him out.

THE TRUE HISTORY OF MASTER FARD MUHAMMAD

The Heavens and the Earth belongs to black people, and this is why this teachings has come to you; it is to acquaint you into the knowledge of your own.

I warn those of you who are reading this book, that the time is now right and is at hand, that everything, everything of good or bad must be made known. We are living in the end of this world, the judgment of this world. These are the days of judgment mentioned in the Bible as the "Days of the Judgment" or the "Days of the Resurrection of the Dead," these days represent years and not just little 24 hour days as we know them today, but they mean years. We are in those days now. The coming of Allah and the teachings of Islam to we who have been lost from our kind, native land and our country for the past 400 years means we are in the time of judgment. God doesn't come until the judgment or until the end of the world of Satan. As you have it written in the Bible, prophesied throughout the Bible and also absolutely mentioned in Thessalonians, that God comes after the working of Satan, the devil.[61] After he has done all that he possibly can do of evil, God comes and gives him the freedom to try and take all the people with him to hell if possible.

These are the days that we are now living in. I want you to understand me, my dear people. You are not in accord with the truth; you have not actually believed it. Your time has come, even if you would just turn to Almighty God, you would enjoy salvation or heaven in this world, and in the hereafter you are assured of heaven. Even in this life, God gives the righteous peace of mind and contentment. He is the protector of the righteous after He makes His appearance. The judgment will come and there will be a great separation at the judgment. This is true, but you don't believe that you are living in this time, that there is a great separation now in the workings.

When you first heard that there was someone in your midst giving names similar to foreign or Indian names, such as Karriem, Biarh, Muhammad, Farrakhan, Hassan, Hasim, and Ali, and many other names that you are now hearing, you were so dead to the knowledge of self, kind and to the knowledge of truth and the true God, that you don't even pay any attention to it; moreover, you make fun of these names, because you never heard of these names before. You're called foolish or fools in the Bible and the Holy Qur'an. You should be grabbing a dictionary to see what does these certain names mean. You would learn that these names mean good names of God. As mentioned in mostly all teachings of religion, that God has 99 names and the 100th is Allah That means all the names of good and that they will be saved. The people, it is true, who hold fast and don't loose their salvation by hating to hear the real truth of these names, they will be removed out of the area where there will be war between God and the devil. Only the people who opposes Him, God will fight and bring to naught. It is not the people who do not oppose God and do not teach other people to oppose Him, but it is that vicious and evil people who teach against the belief in Almighty God and teach other people to hate those who believe in Almighty God Allah. These are the people that will receive the severe judgments of God; I warn you my people, since I see that you don't understand too well. You should come to the knowledge of the truth.

God offers you His own name. Every attribute of His name means something glorious, worthy, and something of divine. Not one of His names can be interpreted other than something of divine, but you have the name of the devil: Johnson, Williamson, Culpepper, Hog, Bird, Fish and what not. These are nothing but common devil names. Your Bible teaches you that in that day, God will call you after His own name.[62] They must have the name of the beast taken away from them and given the name of God, before they ever could see the hereafter. Well, this is the time. You hear my name called Muhammad. Go check the devil's dictionary. Read the meaning of it, and he will bear witness to me that it means one that is praised and is praised much and is worthy of praise. It is the name of God, Himself. God is One that is worthy of praise and is praised much.

I say my friend, today you are getting the names of God and you don't even have the knowledge to appreciate it. The devil looks at you and laughs at you holding on to his old no good name, which has no meaning. These Muslim names will live like the sun. There's no such thing as an end coming to these names, but there will be an end to the names of the wicked, the Caucasians.[63] They are the devils. They are the enemy of all Black people. They are the enemy of God and all of His prophets. Anytime you want to know whether this is true or not, read the history of the prophets who have went among white people. Then study all of the good men that spoke up for you that were among them. What happened to them? The white race persecuted them, beat them up, sent them to prison and then killed many of them.

Islam is not a religion. We call it a religion, but it's not a religion, because it is the nature of us; therefore, the nature of us can't be called a religion. That's why the 30th chapter and the 30th verse of the Holy Qur'an teaches you that Islam is not a religion, but it's the nature in which we were born.

If you go to higher Masonry, they will ask you if you were you made a Mason, you'd better not tell them that you were made one; you've got to tell them that you have always been that.

The Holy Qur'an is a true and a righteous book all over the 196,940,000 square miles of earth and water. It's a true book. This is the book you should try and study. Don't go get Seale's translation; don't get no missionary of white peoples' translation of the Holy Qur'an to look for truth, they will deceive you. They don't want you to be Muslims. As you have proof of that today, you'll be persecuted, you'll be sent to prison again and again for accepting Islam, that's the truth. Of course, you go for accepting Christianity. As I told you, they, by nature, are made to be against you. You could be their best follower, that don't make any difference. As along as you're a Blackman that's it; they are your enemy.

The Bible and the Holy Qur'an is referring to you and me if we sum up the teachings of all three scriptures, the Torah, the Gospel and the Holy Qur'an. They all refer to you and I. Using other peoples history to teach you of your own. Think over it my friend.

The poor lost member of the aboriginal Black Nation has now been found and is now guided by God himself so that the Bible's prophesy may be fulfilled; wherein, it say's in Ezekiel, "I will go after them; I will search for them, until I have found them. I will free them." right? "Even I myself, I will go and search for them."[64]

A parable was made of Solomon, and of the great architect who had built a beautiful Temple, then he was killed. Here

33

Solomon [symbolically] acts as the God: He sends searchers for him to find where had he fallen dead at. When the searchers, returned they said, "We found him, but we could not raise him, he was so rotten that his flesh slipped off his bones. He had been dead a long time; nevertheless, we found a sign of life in his grave growing up from his grave, we see the sign of life.

The Bible says: "Though dead, yet shall he live."[65] You must know the truth. "He's dead, yet he shall live." Again, "Those that die in the Lord shall live again, hence forth,[66]" says the spirit. The spirit of prophecy, referring to a people that will loose the knowledge of themselves and of their God. Don't consider them to be absolutely hopeless, for they will live again, they will live again.

How was he killed? "The enemy killed him by knocking him in his head." So if he was struck in the head, this is the real place to kill the man. Solomon said, "I will go and see if I can help you raise him." He went himself to show them how to get a hold of a dead man. Regardless to how secret you made it, it is the truth. It symbolizes the real people of today. He showed the people how to raise this man, how to take hold of the dead, after they had taken him up out of the grave. He directed that the dead man be buried under the Temple. He had been taken East and they found him in the West.

I say to you my friends, many have attempted to solve your problems. Many have come here trying to raise you; you were too dead here. They couldn't raise you, but now the Father have come. The King of Peace has come and He taught me [Elijah Muhammad] how to get a hold of you. He said to me, "You must rise, for the time is at hand." You must rise, it is written. Look in your own Bible, it is time. The Bible teaches you itself that it is time that the dead should arise. "Stand him up, put him on the square, turn his face back to his people and to his native land, then he will be upright, then he will be forever successful from then on. Take him up."

While they were searching for the body, they heard someone in the bushes groaning. Those who had killed that fine architect was groaning and moaning. They were in agony over committing such evil. "Woe to me that I have ever brought such a man here. I'm sorry, I'm sorry, but if your problems are not solved, America will say, "Woe to us for ever bringing such a people as this to us, and for our evils that we have did against them."

I will tell you of that which I know for myself. I have had priests come to me and say, "I'm sorry." He said, "We feel that we have mistreated you all and we would like to do something about it," but the time is right that you must rise.

Poor Marcus Garvey, a hard working man, he wanted so see you into your own, trying to buy ships to take you back to your own, which wasn't necessary. If you're not given up and put back into your own land and among your own people, your stay here will not be doing any good to America. No, No, and the wise man of America knows that; for God himself have found you and God himself is after you and He's not going to let America rest nor will He let you rest until He has put you back into your place. Go after your own. Seek your own God. Seek your own religion, the religion of peace. You are a most beloved people. God just loves you, because you are nothing and He want to make something out of you. It is not that you are so great, no, you're nothing. It is not that you are so good,

35

no, you are evil yourself, but God just want to fulfill that which He put in the mouth of His prophet: that He would come after you after 400 years of enslavement[67] and He would take you back and put you in your own native land. The world knows that, you are the only people that don't know it. But I'm telling you.

Once I was a Mason too until I became a Muslim. I was a Mason. You must remember that the Holy Qur'an teaches that a Muslim or Moslem is the brother of the Muslim. You must remember the scripture or the rituals that they use concerning a lost architect, think over it. If we are studying that and learn what it means and who it actually really is, then I say you are wise. You must remember my friend that these things all now has come to light.

There is a prophesy in the Bible that "He," meaning God, will send His Angels, send His people, from the East to gather you from the West.[68] A Saviour has been born. I will go after him, even I. I will search for him until I find him. When I find him, I'm going to take him back to his own people. He reached out and made a prophecy against the fall of Israel: "I'm going to plant it on the hills, on the mountains of Israel.[69]" Don't look for earth, it's the rulers and the authority of that nation: the mountains of Israel. Israel [was] "voted" up as rulers of the people. "I'm going to mount you up and make you the ruler of self and others. I'm going to search for them." They have to be searched for, why? "An enemy has them and the enemy is hiding them. The enemy calls them by his name. They don't know Me. They are not as wise as a donkey: the donkey knows his master, but My people do not know Me." Think over it. "I'm going to search for them; for an enemy has them and an enemy is hiding them. "They don't know Me, because the enemy didn't teach them of Me. They don't go in their own peoples' names; they don't pray the prayer of their people; they don't turn their faces toward the East; they don't spread out their hands to Me as I teach them. I must go after them; I must save them from such people." What are you going to do with such people? "I'm going to turn them over to their own kind. I'm going to choose them; they're going to be My people; I'm going to make for Myself a Nation."

Who could or who should be any happier than you and me, that a Saviour was designed to come to save us. What are we in trouble with? "The time has come, as I give it to Abraham, that I'm going to judge that people,[70]who kept us slaves for 400 years. I'm going after them. I'm going to free them [Blacks] again and I'm going to judge that people. I'm going to announce judgment and death to them, because they have destroyed My people. They have robbed them; they have spoiled them; they have blinded them; they can't see all the way.

I'm happy to say that he has been found due West. He must be restored; he must be taken back in the Temple of his own. The Temple of which he was the architect. He must be carried home. So I'm happy to say to you that all of these things are now coming true in your own history. You are the answer to it all. You're Hiram Abif yourself. Yes sir, you are the one. You are the one that has been hit in the head, and it takes a long time for that head to heal. You are the one. You are the one that needs to be stood up. I say my friend, you are the one that has the blindfold on. You are the one that ought to be crying for light and more light, but you are not. You're reaching for the blindfold. Stand up my friend for self and know that you're in the day that you must be separated from the people that you have known for the last 400 years. God doesn't lie. He doesn't allow his prophets to lie. It is written and it must be fulfilled: you must go back to your own.

I think the white people here have done a great thing for you and I. They have not driven you out of the country. They have tried to give you jobs. They have tried to feed you when you didn't have nothing to do, is that right? That's the truth. Give credit where it's due. They're still trying to feed you and you're out of work today. Look at the unemployment line around on the streets. They are out there now by the hundreds, is that right? He doesn't have any work for you to do; yet, you won't go to your own. It is like the book said Lazarus was: he just wouldn't leave the rich man's gate. He stayed there until the rich man died himself.

I say my friend, I have God on my side to bring you into a better condition. I have God on my side to bring you into a land of your own, a home of your own where you won't be giving other people a headache in their home and where you won't have a headache trying to find a home where there is no home for you.

This is the end of the white man's world. It could be the end of the Blackman's world if he wants to sit down and do nothing. Naturally you will soon come to an end if you don't do something for yourself, that is, if no one else is not doing it for you. As I told you three or four years ago in the paper, you cannot always depend on the white people to carry you. You didn't believe it. Now the day is fast coming that he's about to tell you, he soon will tell you, "I just can't carry you, that's all, don't have nothing for you to do". And if he tells you that, what can you say? "Well I helped make the bread for you, now you don't want to give me none". But brother, if he tells you to go for yourself, that you are free, now get on out and look over this earth for a living for yourself - can you blame him? Will you blame an old mule if you open the locked gate and tell that mule, "There is green grass out there mule - go eat, help yourself," and that mule will not go out to eat, but still stands there licking the trough, it will make you angry with the mule.

In reading a book in Washington Congressional Library on Ancient Masonry, I had to laugh sometimes to see how we have been fooled. And now you'll get their highest degree in that order which no white man would ever teach you.

If we bring to you (I'm talking about the disbelievers and hypocrites), that Flag and tell you that it is our sign or emblem, you that have studied degrees in Masonry should not hesitate to come over, because we give you more than what the devil has given you. These brothers (FOI) sitting here before our eyes and controlling the [floor and spaces], they are men that have learned more about Masonry than you. Your Masonry has included the history of your slavery, and it also teaches you that, but you don't know it. Your first three (3) degrees takes you into your slavery. Those three degrees there, are the answer to your slavery, if you understand. But not understanding them, as the white man would not teach you the theology inside of it, it makes you dumb to even that which you actually own. I don't like to call you such names, but it's an easy answer to the truth of it. You look, the ignorant among you, at that [Flag of Islam] and laugh at it, because he's ignorant of the truth of it. He doesn't know what he's doing. He'll smile at his old stars and stripes, he calls it "Old Glory." If I were you, I'd change the name and say it's "Old Hell."

THE TRUE HISTORY OF MASTER FARD MUHAMMAD

I'm positive that if you would let me teach you, you'll go out
sticking out your little chest. It will make you feel like sticking
your chest out, but I say don't act proud; be humble and yet
commanding. If we bring to you the Sun, Moon and Star and
you laugh at it, criticize it, and say you don't want it and say
that you'd rather have a made square of the devil and that that's
enough for you to get by, you're only wishing to become
recognized by the devil, not by you and your people. That is
why you go and you join up with them in every society that
you think he'd let you in. You want to be his equal, be
recognized and respected by him. He didn't make his society
or societies to make you his equal. He robbed you of money
alright enough to be called one of them. He don't like calling
you no "brother" in no society. Now before we will tell him
that we will accept him calling us "brothers," he tries to call us
"brothers." Many white people out there call us "brothers" or
refers to us as "the brothers," because we have the truth and the
right act and in our right position of the square. We don't do
this for forms or fashions, no; it is the truth. If we say that we
are "on the square with you," that doesn't mean that we're just
saying that because the sign is a Square. No; we say that,
because we are "the Square" ourselves. Not that we make a
sign to go by, we're the Square, and we are the Star, and we are
the Moon. You do these things according to his teachings just
for the respect of the whites who are one. They are getting
recognition of it in America and then Australia and into
Europe. This is just a act that they have for you to buy to get
among them. Freemasonry, even in itself, does not take you
any further than Australia and into Europe. But this [Flag of
Islam] takes you all over the Earth.

I want you to wake up and know yourself to be people of the
first order, not of the last order, but of the first order. We are to

respect each other as brothers and not as enemies. We are to respect our woman as our mother. I say my friend, this means that we have to love each other. We can't do these things if we hate each other. That's why we are very careful with you. The devil has put poison in your mind against self and love of yourself, and hoping you can be like him. Hope that you don't be like him. These people were made for hellfire. They were made to live only to a certain time. He tells us himself. Some places he goes, the children of the natives see him and say "There goes a foreign devil." They know him better than you. A real devil is one that is made by nature of evil; his very nature, the material which he's made. I do not use the word create, because he is not from the creation. He's a made man that our scientist, Yakub, made here 6,000 years ago. But we have been on this earth every since it was created.

Blackman remember you are the father of creation. Black man remember that no white man can dispute with the one who said it, Elijah. He can't dispute with me; I'm a God taught man; I am a God raised man. I wear this on my head (Sun, Moon and Star), but we allow the white man to wear it publicly, but once a year. You know why he can't wear it over once a year? Because he has nothing to do with the making of it. The Blackman made this fez. What I mean is, the Sun, Moon and Star. The white man knows nothing about the creation of such planets. This is why I want to teach you the theology of it. Many things in the universe, many things on earth about human beings and the life of any kind. I'm here to tell you what Allah has taught me of it, not what I know, it is Allah's. The One Who has taught me and I don't think you will be able to make Him out [as telling] other than the truth.

41

The Mystery Of Hiram The Widow's Son

The Masonic ritual of the death of Hiram, the Widow son, has no record in the great light of Masonry, the Bible. It is the symbolic reminder of the deviltry carried on by the devil in most recent history.

This part of the Masonic ritual was added in 1725, along with the book of the Masonic Constitution prepared by the Rev. Jones Anderson. The proof of the absence of the story in their Bible as a true happening may be found in the Bible 1st Kings 7th chapter, 13th verse. You will see there that Hiram finished the work he was suppose to do for Solomon, yet according to the ritual of the third degree (death of Hiram) you will notice that Hiram was still putting work on the trestle board for the fellow craftsmen when he was attacked by the Ruffians: Jubelo, Jebula, Jubelum. These three are symbolized as ENGLAND, FRANCE AND AMERICA.

The east gate is Africa, the west gate is the West Indies, and the north corner of the Temple is North America.

The U.S.A., England, and France did enslave the Black man, but America is the one who killed him, by fixing him so he would not have any knowledge of himself, and then gave him the name Negro and buried him in the graveyard of the King James version of the Bible.

The fact that he was hit in the head with a setting maul, shows that in the head he died, so that he is mentally dead. Because of this fact, a name was made up for him from the Greek language to fit him (Necro) also spelled (Negro), this word means dead. However, the Germanic inflection in the mixed tongues, the "C," was pronounced as a "G," and Necro became Negra in the south and Negro in the north of the country.

The Blacks under the English and French have never lost their identity, but the poor Black man in America had all his language and history and true religion taken from him. To do this, the men of his nation were murdered and the women left widows. This left a widow nation and we were his sons. However, the ritual of Free-masonry stated that Solomon raised the widow son, after he had been dead for four days. The Hiram of the building of the temple, the Freemason have to represent.

Now the Hiram of their ritual is not really Hiram, it only pretends to be symbolically; so these men call each other Brother Hiram. You are able to attract their attention by speaking to them in a low voice saying, "Hiram," they will jump as if they were hit with a flat edge of a sword, and if you see their ring say, "I see that you are a traveling man." He will talk as long as you don't press him too hard to talk about Masonry openly. And remember, he is under an oath of secrecy. He may show anxiety and will talk.

"CHRISTIAN MINISTRY OF FREEMASONRY"

90% of the ministers of the Protestant world are members of the Masonic order, and is something to be appalled at when you know what is going on in the Masonic Lodge, especially when we see that he is a Mason, and is a follower of the devil in their rituals. I am speaking of the devils, the Black preachers, the Catholic Church, the so-called holy and otherwise, have their own form of worship of Allah (the

Blackman) in such orders as the Knights of Columbus, and the order of Alhambra.

"THE FEZ"

Let us consider the Protestant minister who darns the drawer and cabletow and hoodwink of the Masonic brotherhood. Here we see a man who teaches the people of his audience the only way to salvation is through Jesus Christ, and that the people must be baptized in the name of the Father, the son and the Holy Ghost (whatever that is). They must believe that Jesus died for their sins. Yet, he goes to the Masonic lodge and declares himself to be a poor blind traveler searching for the light with a rope around his neck in bondage. Within the lodge he takes part in rituals that purposely exclude the name of Jesus, and his title "Son of God" and secretly darn the Fez worn by those who believe that only (Allah) is to be worshipped.

The very next Sunday, there he is back in church telling the ignorant people about how Jesus died for their sins. What kind of crazy hypocrisy is this? He teaches about that loving God who gave His son to die for the people and at the same time the minister wears the ring of a traveling man.

The Coming of The Great Mahdi Chapter 3

I will teach you the truth as I have received it from Him Who is the Author of Truth, regardless to whom or what, for I speak not of myself, for I too, was once blind, deaf and dumb, but I speak and write that which I have received of Him (Allah), and on Him do I rely.

There is no mentioning of Jesus in the history of Moses.[71] This cannot refer to the Jesus of 2,000 years ago, nor in the book of Isaiah.[72] For you disbelievers and blind guides who want me to prove what I teach, take a look at his history as recorded in the Holy Qur'an Sharrieff,[73] and try comparing it with the Bible's birth of Jesus.

When the angels said: "O Mary, surely Allah gives you good news with a word from Him (of one) whose name is the Messiah, Jesus, Son of Mary, worthy of regards in this world and the hereafter."

NOTE: In the verse above, Jesus is called according to Arabic transliteration "Al-Masih, Isa and Ibn-i-Maryan," meaning in English, the Messiah, Son of Mary. "Masih," says the commentator on the language, means either one who travels much or one wiped over with some such thing as oil, the same word as the Aramaic "Messiah," which is said to mean, the anointed. If the name means one who travels much, it could not refer to the Jesus of two thousand years ago who spent his life in the small state called Palestine.

45

One of the main things that one must learn is to distinguish between the history of Jesus two thousand years ago and the prophecy of the Jesus 2,000 years ago, which often proves to be that of the Great Mahdi, the Restorer of the Kingdom of Peace on Earth, Who came to America in 1930 under the name of Mr. W. D. Fard. Later, he'd admitted that he was Mr. Wallace Fard Muhammad, the One Whom the world had been looking for to come for the past 2,000 years. According to the Holy Qur'an's chapter and verse which we have under discussion, the name Messiah, the meaning—fits that of the Mahdi more than any other man.

The Mahdi is a world traveler. He told me that He had traveled the world over and that He had visited North America for 20 years before making Himself known to us, His people whom He came for. He had visited the Isle of the Pacific, Japan and China, Canada, Alaska, the North Pole, India, Pakistan, all of the Near East and Africa. He had studied the wild life in the jungles of Africa and learned the language of the birds. He could speak 16 languages and could write 10 of them. He visited every inhabited place on the earth and had pictured and extracted the language of the people on Mars and had a knowledge of all life in the universe. He could recite by heart the histories of the world as far back as 150,000 years and knew the beginning and end of all things.

The name Christ, Jesus, Jehovah, God, Allah and many other good names, rightly are His names and He came to give divine names to the whole of the 17 million so-called Negroes. Jesus was made an example for the Jews.[74] Jesus and his mother were made as a sign.[75]

We know that most all white menfolk love to insult the black women; it is the nature of that race to destroy the black. Mary's father told his daughter that when she went out to care for the stock, to wear his clothes. He made her a beard out of a goat's beard to wear so that the filthy-thinking devils would think that it was he (the father of Mary).

After giving his daughter his instructions on how to protect herself against the insults of the devil, while he was visiting the new construction of a mosque, he took leave of home for three days. After the father's departure, just at the time to feed the stock, there arose a great dust storm (dust cloud) which blotted out visibility. Under this darkness she became afraid to venture out, so while thinking of how the stock would be fed, she thought of Yusuf (Joseph), the only man that she could trust and the only one that she ever loved.

She called him to come and go with her to feed her father's stock. Joseph came in answer to her call. On his arrival at the home of Mary, she showed him the old man's clothing and the goat's beard that she was to wear in her father's absence; but Joseph suggested to Mary to allow him to wear her father's clothes and the goat's beard, and that she wear her own clothes as usual so that the infidels would think that he (Joseph) was the old man (Mary's father). So Joseph and Mary went together from that day on until the return of the old man three days later.

Mary asked Joseph to return after the first day, and on the second day she asked Joseph: "What about your wife, what will she think of your coming here?" Joseph said, "I will tell her that I am working, building an infidel a house," as he (Joseph) was a carpenter. Mary said, "What if your wife says to you, "Where is the money?" This question Joseph had no answer for, so Mary gave Joseph some money to carry home with him (just in case). On the third day, the old man returned. About three months later, he began to notice his daughter taking on weight.

He asked her, "Mary, what have you been eating? You seem to be taking on weight."

She denied that there had been any change in her eating. The old man, her father, went on for a while and became very suspicious as he kept noticing Mary's continued increase in weight. Again he said to Mary: What has happened?" Mary denied not and said: "Father, do you remember when you left home to go to the building of the new mosque?" The father said, "Yes." She said: "Well on that day when you left a dust cloud arose and there was darkness; I was afraid to go out in such darkness to feed the stock, so I called Joseph to go with me, so he came and he did go with me that day and help feed the stock; and also the next day, until you came home."

Her father said: "Yes, it looks like he fed them plenty." And she said: "And this is why I am like this. I told you that I loved Joseph and while alone together, this is what happened. Now I have told you the truth. You may kill me or do as you please."

The father, listening to such confessions from his daughter felt real bad, for the law was the same then as it was in the time of Moses and the Jews and as it is today in the dominant Muslim world. If an unmarried girl is found to be pregnant out of wedlock, she must be killed and the killing falls to the lot of the parents.

As time passed, he began hating to look at Mary's pregnancy. He became sick over it and went to bed. He nearly pulled out all of his beard looking and worrying over what to do about his daughter.

So, at this time, an old prophetess (spiritual woman) met Joseph. When this old, spiritual woman met Joseph, she said to him: "Oh, Yusuf (Joseph), you are the father of Maryam's (Mary's) baby." This was a surprise to Joseph, to learn that this old woman knew of his secret visit to Mary, his boyhood and manhood sweetheart, and began to deny his guilt by saying: "No! No! I am not the father of Mary's child!" The old prophetess woman reaffirmed her charge and said: "Oh, yes, you are the father. I have only come to help you. Don't deny the child. He is the one prophesied in the Holy Qur'an as being the last prophet to the Jews. He is going to be a great man, and as long as His name lives, yours, as being His father, will live.

"I have come to teach you how to save and protect him from the Jew's planning; for the Jews will kill the child. They are expecting a prophet from Allah (God) to be born at this time, and if the child is not carefully protected, they will kill it."

Remember the Bible's saying: "Then Joseph, her husband (under the Jews' marital law), being a just man and not willing to make her a public example, was minded to put her away privily." While he thought on these things, behold, the angel of the Lord appeared unto him in a dream, saying: "Joseph, thou son of David, fear not to take unto thee Mary, thy wife, for that which is conceived in her is of the Holy Ghost."[76] Mary was espoused to Joseph before they came together.[77]

This word "espoused," according to the English language, when referred to man and woman—means engaged to be married, or to give in marriage, or to take up and support. In the case of Joseph and Mary, this seems to fit very well; for they were engaged to marry from childhood, but were never married. The child was conceived out of wedlock, for Joseph was already married to another woman and had six children by her, and these children, by his wife, are mentioned.[78] Of course, you will have to be careful about reading what the Bible calls the Gospel of Jesus, because much of it is not authentic truth, and all Bible scholars will agree with me. Much of it is lost as that of the Torah (which they called the Old Testament) or the book of Moses. Of course, we know that the original Torah was one book and the Injil (Gospel) given to Jesus, was only one book. Adding in and out of the truth, by the world writers, has caused so much misunderstanding of just what Allah (God) and His prophets said, that to correct it, Allah (God) has prepared a new book, altogether, for the lost found brother (the so-called Negroes). All the present scriptures, even the Holy Qur'an, have been touched by the hands of the enemies of the truth (the devils).

"Joseph, after hearing from the mouth of the old prophetess, that his son by Mary, was going to be a great man, a prophet, and the last one to the House of Israel (or the white race in general), he confessed that he was the father, regardless of the cost; which by the law, meant death for both him and Mary. But they were for 'a sign of something that was to come,' and Allah (God) said that the old prophetess woman told Joseph to go and confess to Mary's father, that you are the father of his daughter's unborn child. Tell him that the child is going to be the great and last prophet to the House of Israel (the Jews), and that the Jews would try to kill the child. If you will allow me to take care of Mary, it won't happen. Now, I have told you the truth, so if you like, you can kill me. The old man (Mary's father) had the same thought as Joseph. Since the child is to be a prophet of Allah (God), as being the father of Mary, his name also would live; so, he agreed to let Joseph look after Mary."

Then Joseph asked the old man for the use of one of the stalls of his stock. Joseph took and filled the sides of the stall with straw and made a bed for Mary in the center. From the outside, the stall looked as though it was filled with straw. Joseph left a hole through which he could feed Mary, and he was the nurse. In the dominate world of Islam, then and today, the parents teach both the boy and the girl, how to take care of the wife at childbirth. It is not like it is here in this world, where everything, along with yourself, is commercialized.

Joseph rented one of those fast camels, put Mary and her baby on it, and said to the camel: "Take this woman to Cairo Egypt. Hurry! Hurry!" The camel went directly to Cairo with Mary and her child, Jesus.

When Jesus was 4 years old, he began school, and at the age of 14 he had graduated. Jesus was very fast in learning (as Allah taught me).

Jesus and his mother were Aboriginal Egyptians. This may be the reason Joseph sent them to Egypt—so that she would be among her own people, away from the Jews, whose intentions were to kill her child. The Aboriginal Egyptians are people of the black nation, and even the modern people of Egypt, in fact, are all original Asiatic people of the Black Nation. The American so-called Negroes think that they do not have any people, except those who are in the jungles of Africa. The only

51

people who are not members of the Black Nation are the white race.

At the time of Mary's flight to Egypt, the Jew's every intention was on finding and killing the child Jesus. But, once in Egypt, the child was safe. Between the ages of 12 and 14, an old prophet came looking for Isa (Jesus). This old prophet had a knowledge of Jesus' presence and future life. He wanted to get to Jesus to inform him of just what he may expect, and how to protect himself from the evil intentions of his enemies (the Jews). He began going to the school at the time of dismissal to get a chance to meet Isa (Jesus). When the boys started home, this old prophet would walk up and start looking among them for Jesus. On the third day, he pretended to be looking for a certain address and the address was next door to the house where Jesus lived. He asked one of the boys if he knew where it was? While the boys were trying to think just where the place was, another boy looked and said: "Here comes Isa (Jesus). He lives just next door to the number where you want to go. He will take you to it." The boy told Isa (Jesus) of the old man's desire to find the number, so Jesus said to the old man: "Yes, come with me, I know where it is. It is next door to where I live." As Jesus and the old man walked on, alone, the old man asked Jesus what course was he studying. Jesus mentioned mathematics. The old man said to Jesus: "Yes, that is fine. I have a boy going to school taking the same course. Maybe you could help him." Jesus, who loved to teach someone, said: "Yes, I will teach your son." As they neared the address, the old man said to Jesus: "I am not looking for that address; it is you who I have been trying to get to for three days. I had intended to get to talk with you, if I had to fall down in front of you and let you stumble over me." He then said to Jesus: "Do you know who you are?" Jesus answered and said: "I don't know, but I believe I am going to be a great man." The old man said: "Yes! You are the one who, the Holy Qur'an says, will be the last prophet to the Jews. I have come to teach you how to protect yourself. You will finish school and after finishing school, you will return to the Jew's land, and begin teaching them. If you don't know how to protect yourself, they will kill you. I will teach you how to tune in on them, so you can tell when they are planning to come and do you harm."

So, from that day, the old man began teaching Jesus in lessons, how to tune in on people and tell what they were thinking about. By Jesus already being a righteous boy, he learned in three lessons. The old man tested him and asked Jesus to tune in on him and talk with him. (It is not near as hard to receive a message as it is to send one out to a certain person.) Jesus tuned in on the old man and greeted him. The old man returned the greeting and said: "You are fine. Now you are able to take care of yourself. This is what I wanted to teach you. Now, you may go."

Jesus finally made the trip walking from Cairo, Egypt to Jerusalem, Palestine. Just how long it took him, I don't know. By having to stop and teach along the wayside, it must have taken quite some time. Nevertheless, on his arrival, he began teaching the Jews the religion of Islam. The Jews rejected him and what he taught, except for a few.

Jesus, according to Allah (God), never was able to get over 35, or around that figure, to listen to him at one time. They hated Jesus and would refer to him as a liar, and that Moses was their prophet. They would call Jesus names that were so terrible, they can't be described in writing.

There are any number of scriptures in both the Bible and Holy Qur'an that Jesus was a prophet, sent to House of Israel alone. We have no scripture of him teaching anywhere else, but among the Jews. He was not a universal prophet (not sent to the whole world). He made no attempt to teach the Arabs nor the blacks of Egypt or Africa. According to the history of his disciples, none of them carried Jesus' name and teachings into the countries of the black nation.

Paul, one of the greatest preachers and travelers of Jesus' followers, made no attempt to teach the black nation; nor travel into their countries. (I just can't see how the so-called Negroes think that he is their Saviour, when he didn't save the Jews to whom he was sent, and he has not saved the so-called Negroes from the slavery of white Americans). It is really a shame and a crime, worthy of death, for the devils to have tricked my people into the belief of Prophet Jesus being their God and Saviour: a hearer of their prayers, and at the same time, teaching them that they killed Jesus. It just doesn't make sense. May Allah burn such liars from the face of the earth, for deceiving my people, whom they now kill and burn at will, because they know not their God nor even know themselves! It is sickness to listen to our poor people calling on Isa (Jesus) of 2,000 years ago, as though he were alive in their midst; and, they are really sincere. By my Allah (God), I will bring them into the knowledge of truth and of their God, Allah, or die in the effort.

Break the head of falsehood. Confuse and bring to naught his lying missionaries, who have deceived my people with their lies of Allah, His Prophet Isa's (Jesus) birth and death and the scriptures of the prophets. The so-called Negroes want to know why white people hide the truth from them, the answer is, they are the devils and know that one cannot be enslaved who knows the truth.

Allah, the Best Knower, to Whom be praised forever, Who came in the person of Master W. F. Muhammad, said: "That Jesus, after teaching and running from the devils for 22 years, learned from reading and studying the scripture, that he couldn't reform the infidel race. And that they had 2,000 years more to live to do their devilment and deceive the nations of the earth. He decided to give his life for the truth (Islam), which he taught and was rejected for, for the 22 years of his life in Palestine.

One Saturday morning, between 9 and 10 o'clock, he came out on the streets of Jerusalem and saw a small group of people standing under an awning in front of a Jew's store, trying to shelter themselves from the rain. Jesus walked under the awning with the people and began teaching them. As his teaching began to interest the people, the store owner came out and told Jesus to leave, for he was causing him the loss of sales. Jesus said to the Jew: "If you will allow me to continue teaching them here, while it is raining, I will make them buy something out of your store." The Jew agreed for a while. As time passed on, the Jew saw that the people were not buying as he thought they would. The Jew warned Jesus again to leave his store front. Jesus refused, because he had about 35 people, who had gathered to hear him. The Jew told Jesus: "I know who you are and if you don't leave my store, I will call the authorities."

After the Jew called the authorities to come and take Jesus, they sent two officers to arrest him. There was a reward of $1,500 if he were arrested and brought in alive and 2,500, in gold, if he were brought in dead. The two officers wanted this reward, so both ran to take Jesus and arrest him. They arrived almost at the same time. The two laid hands on Jesus and began quarreling over who was the first to lay his hands on Jesus. While arguing over whose prisoner Jesus actually was, Jesus asked the two officers if they would allow him to tell who touched him first. The two officers agreed. Jesus said: "The one on the right touched me about three-tenths of a second before the one on the left." The officer on the left accepted the decision and left.

Then Jesus and the other officer started walking down the street to turn him over to the authorities. While going on, the officer said to Jesus: "Since you came here to give yourself up to be killed, why not let me kill you and you will not feel it, but if I take you to them (the infidel Jews), they want to torture you and make you suffer. I will kill you in an instant and you will never feel death. Furthermore, I will get more for taking you there dead than alive. I am a poor man with a large family. Why not let me get the larger reward since you came to die?" Jesus agreed and said to the officer: "Come and do it." The officer took Jesus to an old deserted store front, which was boarded up to protect the store from possible stones, thrown by boys, that might break the glass. The officer said to Jesus: "Stand with your back against this store front and put your hands up." Jesus, being a brave man and ready to die, obeyed the officer and stretched forth his hands, like a cross (not on a cross, but made a cross of himself).

The officer drew a small sword-like knife from his side (which looks like the American hunting knife). Only this little sword is sharp, on both sides of the blade, to about two-thirds of its length. He plunged the sword through the heart of Jesus with such force that it went clear through and stuck itself into the boards that he was standing against, and left him as a crucifix position. By Jesus having such strong nerves, his death was so instant that the blood stopped circulating at once. Jesus was left stiff with both arms out stretched in the same position as he put them when ordered by the officer. The authorities came and took him from the boards where the knife had pinned Jesus' body. When Joseph heard of his son Jesus' death, he came and got the body from the authorities.[79] He secured some Egyptian embalmers to embalm the body to last for 10,000 years. Joseph wanted the body embalmed to last as long as the earth (petrified), but was not able to pay for such embalming. The Egyptian embalmers put the body into a glass tube filled with a certain chemical, known only to the Egyptian embalmers, that will keep one's body looking the same as when it died for many thousands of years, as long as no air is allowed to enter the tube that the body is in; that is, if they get the body at a certain time. They buried the body in the old city, Jerusalem.

His body lies in the tomb in such manner that it reflects in four different directions. This was done to keep the enemies from knowing in just what direction the real body is lying.

No Christian is allowed to see the body, unless they pay a price of $6,000 and must get a certificate from the Pope of Rome. The tomb is guarded by Muslims. When Christians are allowed to see Jesus' body, they are stripped of weapons, handcuffed behind their backs, and well-armed Muslim guards take them into the tomb. But, Muslims, the brothers of Jesus, can go to see his body at any time without charge.

THE TRUE HISTORY OF MASTER FARD MUHAMMAD

My people, who believe in Jesus as God and the Bible as the True Word of God on face value, have gone to the extreme in their belief, without the least knowledge of the true meanings of what they read and believe. You have been reading the history of Jesus in this book, as it was revealed to me by Allah (God) in person, Whom you can't believe to have been God, because of your total blindness to the reality of God. The truth hurts the guilty.

Jesus and his mother were a sign of the so-called Negroes, the actual lost and found members of a chosen nation's history among the devils, in the last days of the devils' time on earth.

The birth of Jesus (out of wedlock) was a sign of the spiritual birth of the lost-found so-called Negroes in North America, who are out of their own people and country (out of the wedlock of unity) living and mixing their blood with their real enemies, the devils, without knowledge. Yusuf (Joseph) and Mary's childhood love of each other when old enough, was a sign of the love of Allah (God) for the lost-found, so-called Negroes, at the end of the devils' time (6,000 years). The visiting of Mary by Joseph, for three days under the cover of darkness, and in the absence of the father, and under the disguise of Mary's father's clothes and Joseph's wearing a goat's beard, was a sign of how Allah (God), who is referred to in the name "Mahdi," would come under disguise Himself, in the flesh and clothes of the devils,[80] for three days (three years), to get to the lost-found so-called Negroes and start them pregnating with the truth through one of them, as a messenger, under a spiritual darkness.

Isa's (Jesus') birth and death and his history of two thousand years ago, and his mother, are a direct sign of the history of the so-called Negroes here in America. Also, the visit of Allah (God) and the raising of a Messenger from among them are fulfillments of this sign. Why can't you understand?

The fleeing to Egypt of Mary and her baby, to be schooled for His mission, is a sign of you (so-called Negroes). You will be schooled there for twenty years. You will be taught your language and many sciences of your people and your beautiful universe that have never before been taught. You will suffer here a little while longer, but the joy that awaits you will make you forget your suffering here overnight.

I see you on top and not on the bottom any more, for Allah (God) Himself is doing this. Not you, nor I, nor our kind, only by the orders of Allah. Fear not! Neither persecution or death will prevent your rise, those who believe. Allah has said it. It didn't work in the past, nor is it going to work today.
The history of Jesus and His mother is a sign of the history of the so-called Negroes, who have been lost from their people for 400 years—who now are found and must be returned to their own; or else every Western (Christian) government will be brought to a naught by the Great God, Allah, under the name of Mr. W. F. Muhammad, "The Mighty Mahdi, the Son of Man," Allah in person.

As I have said and shown in my articles on Jesus' history, that most of Jesus' history, 2,000 years ago is referring to an apostle in the last days, and not of the past. In several places, it is referring to the suffering of Allah (God) three and one-half years, trying to get to the so-called Negroes under disguise.

Learn, my dear readers, that the prophesied Son of Man, is Almighty God. And, the Christ, long looked for, has come in

59

the person of Master Fard Muhammad, as it is written; "without observation," or "as a thief in the night." The work that I am doing in the midst of you bears witness of His presence; for by no means do I have power of myself to give life to the spiritually dead (so-called Negroes) except it be from Him. You have had and still have the wrong understanding of the Bible. According to the Bible, David in his palms, prophesied that he heard the Lord say unto his lord, "Sit on my right hand until I make thine enemies thy footstool."[81] This prophesy cannot refer to Jesus of 2,000 years ago, for the Jews have not been made Jesus' footstool; which means being brought into submission, and Jesus being made the victor or their conqueror. The "Lord" that David refers to is Almighty Allah (God), and "his lord" is none other than the Great Prophet, coming just prior to the end of the world, whom the wicked will attack to do to Him what they did to the prophets of old. Allah (God) will come to his aid. David, also being a prophet, saw the last prophet to be much greater than himself and calls him "his Lord." Let the so-called Negroes rejoice for they are the ones whose sins will be forgiven and shall be saved.

White Christian America has been so busy trying to keep her slaves (the so-called Negroes) under her foot, sitting, watching, spying on them to prevent them from knowing the truth of this day of our salvation, she has failed to see and learn the strength and power of her enemies. She has boasted that she could police the world and has come pretty near doing so, but failed to see the "bear" behind the tree and the "lion" in the thicket. The sky over her is being filled with her enemies' arms which can be seen with the naked eye. Her scientists are troubled and at their wits end to find time to make ready, as it is written: "I have set the point of the sword against all their gates, that their heart may faint, and their ruins be multiplied. Ah! It is made bright. It is wrapped up for the slaughter." [82]

Answer: "For the tidings: because it cometh, and every heart shall melt and all hands shall be feeble and every spirit shall faint and all knees shall be weak as water." [83]

Who is His father if God is not His Father? God is His Father, but the Father is also a man. You have heard of old that God prepared a body, the expected Son of Man; Jesus is a special prepared man to do a work of redeeming the lost sheep (the so-called Negroes). He had to have a body that would be part of each side (black and white), half and half. Therefore, being born or made from both people, He is able to go among both black and white without being discovered or recognized.

This He has done in the person of Master W.F. Muhammad, the man who was made by His Father to go and search for the lost members of the Tribe Shabazz, though you find them among the infidels, return them to their own. Master W. F. Muhammad is that Son of Man that the world has been looking for to come for 2,000 years, seeking to save that which was lost.

There are no historical records that there was ever a people lost from each other for 400 years other than we, the so-called Negroes. We have been so long separated from each other that we have lost the knowledge of each other. Even today the white American slave-masters are ever on the watch to keep out any Asiatic influence that might come among the so-called Negroes to teach them the truth. They are our real open enemies. This is no secret. The Son of Man is after the so-called Negroes to sit them in Heaven and His enemies in Hell.

THE TRUE HISTORY OF MASTER FARD MUHAMMAD

After His conquest of the black nation's enemies, the world will know and recognize Him (Allah) to be God alone.

There is no problem today that is as hard to solve as the problem of uniting the American so-called Negroes. They are like a dead man totally without life. They have lost all love of self and kind and have gone all out in loving their enemies (the devils). They do not seem to want any God to do anything like blessing them unless that God blesses their enemies too. Fear of their enemies is the real cause.

The time is now ripe that they should have no fear, only the fear of Allah, Who is in person among them to save them from their enemies. By all means, they must be separated from the white race (the devils), in order that the scripture might be fulfilled. "For I will take you from among the heathen and gather you out of all countries and will bring you into your own land." [84]

The so-called Negroes have no home (country) that they can call their own. They have helped the white race (the devils) to own a free country, but they have nothing for themselves. This is the purpose of His coming; to give everyone that which is rightfully theirs. The Son of Man (the Great Mahdi, God in person) has power over all things. You cannot find a defense against Him in war. Your weapons mean nothing. The powers of Heaven and earth today will be ordered to fight on the side of the Mahdi (Son of Man) against His enemies. He is the friend of the so-called Negroes and not of white people. His purpose is to take the so- called Negroes and kill their enemies, although many of us will suffer from persecution and hunger. The good end is for those of you who will hold fast to Allah and His religion, Islam. They (the devils) are now planning many tricks to keep the Negroes here with them to suffer the fire of hell which they (the devils) cannot escape. Fly to Allah! Come, follow me. Although I may look insignificant to you, you will find salvation with us. The white race is excited and cannot think rightly for themselves. The so-called Negroes, Muslims, in their midst are a shelter but little do they know it.

The final war between Allah (God) and the devils is dangerously close. The very least friction can bring it into action within minutes. There is no such thing as getting ready for this most terrible and dreadful war; they are ready! Preparation for battle between man and man or nations have been made and carried out on land and water for the past six thousand years. But, man now has become very wise and knows many secret elements of power from the natural world which make the old battles with swords, bows and arrows look like child's play.

Since 1914, which was the end of the time given for the devils (white race) to rule the original people (black nation), man has been preparing for a final showdown in the skies. He has made a remarkable advancement in everything pertaining to a deadly destructive war in the sky. But Allah, the Best of Planners, having a perfect knowledge of His enemies, prepared for their destruction long ago, even before they were created. Thanks to Allah, to Whom be praised forever, Who came in the flesh and the blood, for more than seventy years making Himself ready for the final war.

Allah, to Whom be Praised, came in the person of Master W. F. Muhammad; the Great Mahdi expected by the Muslims and the anti-Christs (the devils) under the names: Jesus Christ, Messiah, God, Lord, Jehovah, the last (Jehovah) and the Christ.

These meanings are good and befitting as titles, but the meaning of His name "Mahdi," as mentioned in the Holy Qur'an Sharrieff 22:54, is better. All of these names refer to Him. His name, FARD MUHAMMAD, is beautiful in its meaning. He must bring an end to war, and the only way to end war between man and man is to destroy the war-maker (the trouble maker).

According to the history of the white race (devils), they are guilty of making trouble; causing war among the people and themselves ever since they have been on our planet Earth. So, the God of righteousness has found them disagreeable to live with in peace and has decided to remove them from the face of the Earth. God does not have to tell us that they are disagreeable to live with in peace; we already know it, for we are the victims of these trouble makers. Allah will fight this war for the sake of His People (the black people), and especially for the American so-called Negroes. As I have said time and again, we, the so-called American Negroes, will be the lucky ones. We are Allah's choice to give life and we will be put on top of civilization.

Read your "poison book" (the Bible). What does your book say concerning the preparation of God against the devil? Take a look at Ezekiel's vision of it, 595 B.C. "Now it came to pass in the thirtieth year, in the fourth month, in the fifth day of the month, as I was among the captives by the river of Chebar, that the heavens were open and I saw visions of God. Now as I beheld the living creatures, behold one wheel upon the earth by the living creatures, with his four faces. As for their rings, they were so high that they were dreadful; and their rings were full of eyes around about them four." [85]

It was on the fourth of July, 1930, when the Great Mahdi, Allah, in person, made His appearance among us.

How To Understand Jesus Chapter 4

No, Jesus two thousand years ago was not your Jesus. No, by no means. By no means can he save one finger of yours if it was being cut off. No, not that man two thousand years ago. He could not save you if you all were lined up out there before the enemy's gun and was mowed down. He couldn't save one of you. No. Not that man that was here two thousand years ago. I know how you have been taught. Don't tell me how you love him. I know you love him, but I want you to remember that Elijah is telling you that he didn't even come to you. He only prophesied of you being lost in the last day and then he prophesied that God would send you one. All praises due to Allah.

He says to you, according to the Bible over here in John, that "The father will send you one. I go away,"[86] meaning I die, but nevertheless, you won't be left without a guide. In that day God will send you one, like he sent me to these devils.[87] God will send you one, but that one who He sends in that day will be the last caller. If you won't hear that man in that day, you won't get away with it as the Jews is getting away with not hearing me.[88] Because that man is going to get it directly from the mouth of God, and the God is going to be with him and he with the God and the God is going to be ready for execution - to execute the wicked. That man in that day and time, he's coming from God. As Moses said, "In that day, the Lord thy God shall raise up from out of the midst of you and of thy brethren a prophet one liken unto me."[89] And if you fail to hear that man, it will be required of you. He will speak that only which he hears.

All prophets in the past came with that right. All prophets in the past, their mission was revealed to them, but according to the prophecy of Moses and Jesus of the last prophet, he gets his guidance directly from the mouth of God. "In that day, I will not write it on parchment, I'm going to write it on the tables of their hearts."[90] Is that right? They all shall know me. Have that ever come to past? If so, it's just coming to past. They all didn't know him in the day of Jesus. No man had seen God at anytime.[91] Is that right? That's what they said in those days. No man has ascended to heaven, but he that came from heaven and returned.[92] Could that have been Jesus? No. Not that Jesus. He didn't come from heaven. He came from Palestine. I'm sure some of you all think that I'm an infidel now, but have patience, this is according to your Bible. Jesus was born in Palestine, in Bethlehem.[93] Now if you declare that he came from some other place other than that, you will have to prove it.

If you preach that he came from heaven then where is that heaven? If you would preach that he came from hell, where was the hell? All praises due to Allah. Don't get impatient. Let's contend with each other on the truth.

If now that he was born in Palestine and of a woman, she had the same conception of that child as other women. And that child lived here and that child was killed and he died and they buried him as other dead bodies. Is that right? "Yeah, but he rose again." All right then, if he came from heaven, then and he was not flesh and blood in heaven and the God only sent him through Mary to get him a body? Hold on preacher there. Let's talk it over a little.

Jesus had gotten his body through Mary. Now, when they kill that body, as the Bible teaches, then he didn't need that body anymore did he? He should enter then back into his heavenly body, because he only had that as a veil or shield to cover that body that he brought from heaven. All praises due to Allah. The Bible said, when he rose, he rose in the same body and even the body was still wounded; and when he left his disciples, they said they saw him ascending up into heaven in the same body that Mary gave him.[94] They didn't see him come from heaven at all, but saw him in the manger[95] and now they have wounded that body and they say that that wounded body is going on up into the heavens and a cloud intervened between them. Is that right? And they said, Jesus went on back to heaven with a body that he got in Palestine. If we are going to take the words [literally], that "no one has seen God; no one has been to heaven, but he that came from heaven and sent back." Well then, if he didn't bring that body from heaven, he robbed us [on earth] of a little something. Is that right?

I know you want to call me an infidel so bad, but reason with me. I'm just preaching your Bible. We didn't see him come down from out of the clouds to Mary did we? All right then, if we didn't see him coming out of the sky to Mary; yet, Mary had produced him, [then why is] he going up in the sky with part of Mary's body? You know that the average of our people don't like Elijah, because Elijah puts this thing to them so strong, and when they can't find an answer, then they hate him for it. Don't hate me because you cannot find an answer. That's not my fault. If you have the truth then prove it.

THE TRUE HISTORY OF MASTER FARD MUHAMMAD

My beloved brothers and sisters, you have misunderstood the Bible. You have misunderstood the history of Jesus, and the white man likes your misunderstanding. They like it, because it keeps you a slave to them. My friend, it was nothing of the kind.

That body that Jesus was killed in has not left the earth. It's still on the earth. It's embalmed over there in Jerusalem to last eight thousand years longer than the two thousand years, and it will be there eight more thousand years.[96] The Egyptians embalmers[97] hired by his father Joseph, his real earthly father. Now you can name him the other father if you want, but that was his real earthly father.[98]

Now that you believe that Jesus was a man of flesh and blood, born of a woman as you and I were; and that that flesh was wounded by a knife that brought death to Jesus and the same wounded flesh then came to life again and was seen going up in the sky of its own accord, until the view was shut out by clouds, this is the wrong way to believe, and understand that Bible story of Jesus. Nearly 75 per cent is referring to a future Jesus, coming at the end of the white races' time, to resurrect the mentally dead, lost members (so-called Negroes) of the tribe of Shabazz. This Jesus is now in the world.

Jesus and his mother were made a sign of something to come, and we are the end or fulfillment of that sign. "And we made the Son of Mary and his mother a sign."[99] There are some who think that the sign refers only to the Jews, in the sense that Jesus was the last of the Prophets; not only to the Jews, but to white race in general. We must not forget that Jesus was not a member of that race. Jesus belonged to the black nation.

In order to make the American so-called Negroes worship the devils, the American devils paint Jesus, God and the Angels white. Many of the so-called Negroes take these imaginary pictures as real; while there is not a real picture of Jesus, nor his disciples. The foolish American so-called Negroes have worshipped the devils (white race) all of their lives. Now, today, he will openly dispute with you that Jesus was a white man (a Jew); not taking the time to think, that if Jesus was a member of that white race, he would have been a devil. Again, Jesus would not have declared that the Jews were devils (John 8:44).[100] This chapter should convince the so-called Negroes, that the white race can't love and do good by them. They are not from the God of goodness, mercy and truth.[101] Jesus also condemned them in claiming Abraham to be their father.[102]

The white races' work, their open hatred of us, their murdering and killing of you, me, themselves and the righteous, proves beyond a shadow of a doubt, that they are the real devils. They actually love the making of war, persecuting and killing the so-called Negroes; worst of all, they make the frightened so-called Negroes help them war against those whom they term to be their enemies; while they are the worst enemies of the Negroes on earth. They openly tell the so-called Negroes that they will not give them equal justice with themselves. They will go to war against any few who attempt to give the Negroes justice.

The so-called Negroes see all of this going on against them; yet, love and desire to destroy themselves with such enemies, rather than follow me to their own God and people, with whom they will be given equal love and justice. They (so-called Negroes) even hate me for teaching the truth, due to their ignorance of truth.

71

THE TRUE HISTORY OF MASTER FARD MUHAMMAD

My people (the so-called Negroes) should be real happy after reading the truth in this book that God has revealed to me, seeing that the salvation belongs to them and not to the Jews, as they have been made to believe.

It is a pity that they have been made so blind, deaf and dumb, to the extent that in order to make them believe the truth, Allah (God) will have to whip them into submission. That is why I am teaching them night and day, for the chastisement of Allah is to be feared even by the devils.

Beware, my people! Do not take what I am writing here as a joke or mockery. It is the divine truth, from the very mouth of God, and not a made-up story of myself. I have not the brains to think up such truth. I once was as dead as you are. Don't give me any credit for Allah's (God's) revelation of truth to me (even you who believe). Give praises to Allah, to Whom it is due, for I am only your brother and a sufferer with you, under the same. If you would believe in Allah (God) as I do, though under your burden, you would feel it not.

So many of you are writing and asking almost the same questions. If you continue to read my articles you will find the answers to all of your questions.

The Holy Qur'an and the Muslims have great respect for Jesus, but not as God. He was only a prophet. "He (Jesus) was naught but a servant, on whom we bestowed favor, and we made him an example for the children of Israel." [103] Here he is mentioned as being an example for Israel; and he was, in the way of a true Muslim (righteous). An example of a doer of righteousness and obedient to the law of Allah as Moses had given them.

Israel was never a doer of the law. The 57th verse of the same chapter refers to what the Christian-believing black people here (the so-called Negroes) will say to Muhammad. "And when the son of Mary is mentioned as an example, lo! the people (the so-called Negroes) raised a clamor (a loud out-cry; uproar; vehement expression of the general feeling)."

This is true of the shameful way the so-called Negroes carry on over the name or mentioning of Jesus in churches and public places, as though Jesus is present and looking on. Poor people. I hope to bring you out of such ignorance of Jesus. He was only a prophet and is dead like Moses and prophets of old. None can hear your prayers. You must pray to a living Jesus, or God, if you want your prayers answered.

Just be faithful and clamorous over the real Jesus of today; and you will surely go to Heaven with Him. The false doctrines of Jesus being God were introduced after His death.

And when Allah will say; "Oh, Jesus, Son of Mary, didst thou say to men: "Take Me and My mother for two gods besides Allah?" He will say: "Glory be to Thee; it was not for Me to say what I had no right to say, if I had said it, Thou wouldst indeed have known it. Thou knowest what is in my mind and I know what is in Thy mind. Surely Thou art the great knower of the unseen. I said to them naught save as Thou didst command Me. Serve Allah, my Lord and your Lord; and, I was a witness of them so long as I was among them, but when Thou didst cause Me to die, Thou wast the watcher over them, and Thou art witness of all things.

73

"If Thou chastise them, surely Thou art the mighty, the wise."[104]

Remember the Bible teaches that Jesus was dependent upon His Father (God) in these words: "I can of Mine own self do nothing: as I hear, I judge: because I seek not mine own will, but the will of the Father which hath sent me." [105] God is not sent, nor does He depend on instructions from anyone. A prophet is sent with a message and is dependent on his sender for guidance. So Jesus was in every respect, even after His resurrection. He didn't claim to be God. "Touch me not: for I am not yet ascended to My Father." [106] "And now I am no more in the world, but these (His followers) are in the world, and I come to Thee, Holy Father, keep through Thine own name, those whom Thou hast given me, that they may be one, as we. While I was in the world. I kept them in Thy name." [107]

Compare the above with the 5:117 of the Holy Qur'an. Jesus declared that He is no more in the world and cannot be witness of what His followers will do; nor be responsible for them after his death.

No prophet is responsible for the people after he fulfills his mission to them or dies in the attempt. Study your book and understand the truth before you dispute with me. Jesus was only a prophet and is dead like Moses and the other old prophets. Pray to a living God and come follow me, and He will hear your prayers.

History repeats itself. The same race that hated Jesus 2,000 years ago hates Jesus' people (the so-called Negroes) today, and is casting them out. The limited knowledge that the so-called Negroes have of themselves and their enemies makes them think that the enemies' rejection of them is wrong, but is not.

It is really their salvation to be rejected by the devils. The wrong that the enemies are doing to you is not letting you go free. Indeed, they won't allow even Allah (God) to do so without war. They won't teach you the truth of self, God, devil or the true religion.

They persecute and kill you without justice. They put fear into you, and that fear makes you harmless like sheep before a pack of hungry, merciless wolves, who stay in your family after the so-called Negro women.

The poor people (so-called Negroes) and their foolish leaders (preachers) should visit and join onto your own, Islam from the cradle to the old man and woman leaning on a stick.

You shout and weep, pity poor Jesus' murder and death at the hands of His enemies 2,000 years ago, but is seems as though you should not cry nor weep over you own selves, being beaten and killed daily. Yet you say nothing nor do anything about it, but love the enemies.

The parable of us under the title "Lazarus laying at the rich man's gate" could not give a better type of the so-called American Negroes.[108]

They just won't go for self, as long as the slave masters are rich and will allow you to be their servants and make rosy promises to you only to deceive you. But today is very serious for you and for them. Think well and wisely for your future.

Allah (God) and his religion, Islam, are your only friends. The white race is not able to help itself against Allah. So your believing and seeking a future in the race, today, is like one seeking shelter under a spider's web from a storm of hailstones.

The mother of Jesus well represents a messenger from among you, pregnation with a new world out of you.

Almighty God, Allah, is the Father and must protect the infant "baby nation" (the so-called Negroes) whom he is carrying.

Jesus, making a clay bird by the permission of Allah, the healing of the sick, giving sight to the blind, raising the dead, teaching the people what they should eat and what they shouldn't eat,[109] means one and the same thing.

The work of the last apostle to the so-called Negroes, who are spiritually blind, deaf and dumb.

They are eating the wrong food and now being taught against the eating of poison foods by the Apostle of Allah. No such work was done among the devils 2,000 years ago. It was not necessary since the devils are not to be saved.

Let me make myself clear to you. I am not trying to condemn the history of Jesus as being false; but, rather am trying to put the meanings and signs, or miracles where they belong. That is, in the present so-called Negroes' history, and Jesus of today. Jesus and His parents were only a sign or prototype of that which was to come.

Of course, there are many student ministers in the theological seminary colleges, who probably know, or are learning, that most of what the Bible gives us of Jesus' history has got to be a future man and not one answering any such description of 2,000 years ago.

How could Jesus' birth and death 2,000 years ago serve as the price of sin and peace (reconciling God and the man of sin), of the world as the average Christian believe? The rejoicing angels at his birth; the mourning and directing angels at His tomb; the great earthquakes; the tense darkness; the seeing of resurrected saints; the going up to heaven in a cloud, as Matthew, Mark, Luke and John gives us in the gospel of Jesus?

It just can't be put in the past without disgracing the All Wise God's intelligent knowledge of the future. Let the poor so-called Negroes' minds relax for a few minutes, while reading this book, and use common sense. (1st) if Jesus were to have a flesh and blood body, He must be produced as we were, by the agency of man, who had flesh and blood. If God produces one other than by man, He breaks His own law. And, we could not be held responsible for breaking the same law (getting children out of wedlock). (2nd) The world has never been without a righteous people on it. Could not God produce a son or prophet from a righteous couple as He had in the past? And, even as He did by Zacharias and his wife, to produce John, who was a little older than Jesus, according to the Bible.[110]

Read the birth and death of Jesus as recorded in Matthew, Mark, Luke, and John. Think it over. Would God have permitted such thing to happen 2,000 years ago with such evil results following afterward? If Jesus' birth was to bring peace and goodwill to all mankind,[111] how could He have prophesied of "Wars and rumors of wars, nations rising against nations, and the hatred of one another?"[112] There have been more wars and more evil since the birth and death of Jesus than ever before. Jesus didn't bring peace to the world, according to the Bible.[113] Elijah comes to unite the family and put them on the path of God, to bring about a union between man and God.[114]

According to the Bible, Jesus taught to "hate every member of the family, even the father and mother."[115] Even God said: "He loved one brother and hated the other brother."[116] You, who preach that God is love and Jesus taught to love one another, should have consulted the translators of the Bible as to just why they charge God's and Jesus' teaching for a thing in one place and against it in another place.

Your Bible is poison, double crossing itself. Be careful how you understand it. We know what it means and where it belongs; but, since you are disbeliever in the truth and disputers without knowledge, we challenge you to prove your sayings by your book, if you have understanding of it.

You have two Jesus' histories, as I have said time and again; and, even an apostle's history of the last days, all under the name of Jesus, 2,000 years ago.

I am so happy that Allah (God) has revealed to me the truth, believe it or not. Oh, you die-hard Christians, who are stubborn and proud against Allah (God), His word, and we who believe in Him and His word, my people are deaf, dumb, and blind; and gravely mislead by the enemy (devil). Use common sense, my people, and judge between the truth, which I am writing, and the false that was taught to you by the devils.

Jesus came as a sign of that which was to come. His birth, ministry, persecution and death were signs of the persecution and death, as I have written, of the future of you (the so-called

Negroes) his people; and the persecution and rejection of the Great Mahdi (God in person) who has appeared among us in these last days of this race of devils, and has suffered the same. Jesus was an example of righteousness, a doer of the law of the Jews, which was given to them by Musa (Moses).

The world, looking for that Jesus to return, is not only ignorant, but foolish. No one, but a fool, would believe that Jesus, who was here 2,000 years ago, is sitting in heaven waiting until his time to return and execute judgment. Tell the world the truth, and stop fooling yourself, if you know it; and, if you don't know it, step aside and stop trying to hinder us, who are telling the truth.

The Bible makes it a little too hard for the average reader to believe in Jesus as a prophet, or a man born by the agency of man, like you and I; though, never did God intend otherwise. The Holy Qur'an makes Jesus only a prophet of Allah (God); and, that is all He was. It does not mention his father by name, though on many occasions, prophets and their great works of the past are mentioned without their father's names. There are many Muslims who think that His birth was without the agency of man. Most commentators, on the life and death of Jesus, disagree with the saying that, "Jesus dies on the cross, or was even murdered (killed)." They think that He traveled into India and died in Kashmir, but this is wrong. He did not go there, nor is that His tomb in Kashmir. It is only an old belief among those who actually did not know who the Nabi (prophet) was, who came to Kashmir and died and was buried there, whom old settlers claimed came from the West. No real proof is shown that it was Jesus' body.

The scholars on the Holy Qur'an go to the extreme with the word "spirit" as the Christians do, especially in the case of Allah. My work is to bring you face to face with God, and to do away with spooky beliefs. The revealing of the spiritual word of Allah (God) to Mary or anyone, does not mean for you and me to believe that Jesus was born without the agency of man. The spirit or word of Allah (God) came to Moses' mother, to inform her about the future of her son (that He was a prophet).[117] Both the Bible and Holy Qur'an seem to be very careful not to accuse Mary of fornication. Why? If she and her son were to be a sign for the nation, she should not be charged with fornication. (2nd) If the act was to serve as a lesson for us, that we should never allow two people who are in love with each other, to be alone together in a place where there are no others, for nature has no self-control. That was the case of Mary and Joseph. They were childhood sweethearts and wanted to be married when of age, but Mary's father objected to it. His objections could not destroy the love between the two. To this day, the Muslims keep boys and girls, men and women, from mixing freely together. Even the boy and girl courtship and marriages are controlled by their parents. There is no fornication, and very little or no divorce cases in the dominant Muslim world. That is why Islam is hated by white Christian devils, because they are not allowed to mix with Muslim women; with their filthy, indecent hearts and winking blue eyes. "We breathed into her of our inspiration, and made her and her son a sign for the nations." [118]

Regardless to the carefulness and chaste language of their scripture used on Mary, having a baby out of wedlock, we can see through it all; after knowledge from Allah (God) in the person of Master Fard Muhammad, to Whom be praised forever. In another chapter it mentions the spirit sent to Mary in the form of a man. "So she screened herself from them. Then we sent to her, our spirit, and it appeared to her as a well-made man."[119]

I am well aware of my disputers, who dispute without knowledge; and who are followers of the devils for certain privileges. They claim to be representatives of God and Jesus, whom they claim to be the Son of God, but are licensed, ordained and sent by the devils. (God-sent men are not licensed, by the world). This class who love to be revered and honored by the people, whether God has any respect for them or not, are really agents for the slave masters (the devils). They are secret persecutors and murderers of the prophets of God, and will say: "If they had been their followers and would not have opposed them;" yet, they persecute me and my followers, and all who teach the truth, for the same things that the enemies of the prophets of old.

It was special privileges that Pharaoh offered the "Enchanters" to oppose Moses as being a liar. "He promised them that they would be drawn near to him," (Pharaoh).[120] It is the nearness (friendship) of the white race that the majority of the so-called Negro preachers seek and not the nearness, love, and friendship of God. They openly confess that in their position (licensed and missioned by the white race to preach according to their liking), they cannot preach the truth if that truth is against the white race. The followers' (church members') burdens are ever made grievous to carry, because of the love and fear of their enemies by the preachers. They call preaching the truth hatred.

Last week, this paper published the hatred of two preachers, of the truth that I am teaching my people in this column. Namely, Rev. Joseph P. King, founder of the International Church of

Chicago, Ill., and Rev. Benjamin F. Reid of Pittsburgh, Pa. Rev. Joseph P. King would like to question the source and extent of my knowledge of what I am teaching.

The source from which it springs, or fountain from which I drink, is the same source from which Noah, Abraham, Moses, and Jesus drank: Almighty Allah (God) of Whom you probably do not believe; as the disbelievers of the above mentioned prophets did not believe in those prophets' truth.

The early man (original man) knew the earth's revolutions; the circulation of blood or the existence of microbes. The only man or people who were late in acquiring such knowledge was the white race; who are the only late or new race we have on our planet. I agree with you on "adherence to the unknown is a throwback to anyone or a nation." This is the number one hold back to the so-called American Negroes. Without the knowledge of self or anyone else, or the knowledge of the God of their salvation, they are strictly adhering or following those who preach and represent a mystery God (unknown), but yet charge that mystery God with getting a son out of wedlock, and He waiting 4,000 years to produce His Son to give His made people (the Adamic race) the religion called Christianity. This is the gravest charge that could be made against the All-Wise, All-Knowing, and All-Powerful God, and they say: "The Beneficent God has taken to Himself a son." Certainly you have made an abominable assertion! The heavens may almost be rent thereat, and the earth cleave asunder, and the mountains fall down in pieces, That they (the Christians' preachers) ascribe a Son to the Beneficent God. And it is not worthy of the Beneficent God that He should take to Himself a Son. There is no one in the heavens and the earth, but will come to the Beneficent God as a servant." [121]

I bear witness with the above said, that an All-wise, All-Powerful God does not need a son and if He would get one as the Christians charge Him, out of wedlock, He then could be charged with adultery. I repeat, "the white man's so-called Christianity is not only no good for the black man, but it is fast proving to be no good for the white race, who are the founders of that religion and not Jesus, as they would like for you to believe."

The great misunderstanding over the Father and Sonship, birth and death of Jesus, is now being made understandable from the mouth of God in person; Whose coming has brought light and truth to us who sit in darkness. The great arch-enemy of Allah and the righteous, the devil in person (Caucasian race), who has deceived us for 6,000 years, took us out of the light of truth into darkness, and now Allah (God), by His grace and power, dispels the darkness and is making manifest this great enemy (the devil). The poor black man of America should rejoice and be glad for this divine truth of Jesus' birth, life, and death, as the real truth of it has never before been told.

Who is this Christ, and His Father that Jesus questioned the Pharisees about? Was Jesus referring to Himself, or another one as Christ? Or does, the above question of Jesus prove that He was the Christ, or that His Father was other than a man? By no means, for according to Joseph's dream[122] concerning the birth of his son, his name was to be called Jesus. "And she shall bring forth a son, and thou shalt call His name Jesus, for He shall save his people from their sins." Did he save the Jews from their sins? They no doubt were not His people according to John (8:42-44). The Jews could not be saved from their sins if their father was the devil, for by nature they were sinners.

Joseph was the husband of Mary and the son of Jacob. In Joseph's dream, he was addressed by the angel as being the son of David.[123] Jesus is called "Jesus Christ," and "Emmanuel." Did the people in those days ever call Jesus "Emmanuel?"[124]

Today, he is called "Jesus, and Christ, the Son of God." Since we have learned that He did not save the Jews from their sins and that he denounced the Jews as being none other than the devil; that He did not restore the independence of the Jews and did not bring peace to the world, nor even to his disciples; nor did He put a stop to death, nor did He destroy sickness from the people, but referred to the Son of Man[125] as having power on earth to forgive sins. He could not have been referring to Himself as the Son of Man who had such power, for He prophesied of the coming of the Son of Man.[126]

The Bible is very questionable, but it can be, and is now being understood, for God has revealed her hidden secrets to me. Such things as "forgiving sins of a special people, nor even as much as healing them; giving spiritual light; resurrection of the dead; bringing peace and goodwill between man and man," could not have been in the days of Jesus 2,000 years ago. Think over it! "Angels coming from heaven to bear witness that he is the One to set up the Kingdom of Peace;" and yet, when he began his ministry, he was dependent on his Father for help, and prophesied of another; the coming of the Son of Man, who would be Self-Independent, having power to restore the Kingdom of Peace on earth and to destroy those who had destroyed the peace and brotherhood of His people."

My greatest and only desire is to bring true understanding of the word of God, His prophets and the scriptures, which the prophets were sent with, pertaining to the lost-found people (the American so-called Negroes) of God, and the judgment of the world.

You must forget about ever seeing the return of Jesus, who was here two thousand years ago. Set your heart on seeing the One that He prophesied would come at the end of the present world's time (the white race's time).

He is called the "Son of Man," the "Christ," the "Comforter." You are really foolish to be looking to see the return of the Prophet Jesus. It is the same as looking for the return of Abraham, Moses and Muhammad. All of these prophets prophesied the coming of Allah or one with equal power under many names. You must remember that Jesus could not have been referring to himself as returning to the people in the last days. He prophesied of another's coming who was much greater than he. Jesus even acknowledged that he did not know when the hour would come in these words:

"But of that day and hour knoweth no man, no, not the angels of heaven, by my Father only."[127]

If He were the one to return at the end of the world, surely He would have known the time of His return: the knowledge of the hour. He left himself out of that knowledge and placed it where it belonged, as all the other prophet had done. No prophet has been able to tell us the hour of the judgment. None but He, The Great, All Wise God-Allah. He is called the "Son of Man," the "Mahdi," the "Christ." The prophets, Jesus included, could only foretell those things which would serve as signs, signs that would precede such a Great One's coming to

85

judge the world. The knowledge of the hour of judgment is with the Executor only.

The prophets teach us to let the past judgment of people, their cities and their Warner serve as a lesson, or sign of the last judgment and its warners. Noah did not know the hour of the flood. Lot did not know the hour of Sodom and Gomorrah until the Executors had arrived, and Jesus prophesied that:[128]

"It will be the same in the last judgment of the world of Satan." You have gone astray because of your misunderstanding of the scripture, the Prophet Jesus, and the coming of God to judge the world. My corrections are not accepted.

Your misunderstanding and misinterpretations of it are really the joy of the devils. For it is the devils' desire to keep the so-called Negroes ignorant to the truth of God until they see it with their eyes. The truth of God is the salvation and freedom of the so-called Negroes, from the devils' power over them, and the universal destruction of the devils' power.

Can you blame them? No! Blame yourself for being so foolish to allow the devils to fool you in not accepting the truth after it comes to you.

The devils have tried to deceive the people all over the planet earth with Christianity; that God, the Father, Jesus the Son, and the Holy Ghost, the three Gods are into One God. The resurrection of the son and his return to judge the world, or that the son is in some place above the Earth, sitting on the right hand side of the Father, waiting until the Father makes His enemies His footstool.

The period of waiting is 2,000 years; yet, he died for the Father to save his enemies (the whole world of sinners).

My friends, use a bit of common sense. First: Could a wonderful flesh and blood body, made of the essence of our earth, last 2,000 years on the earth, or off the earth, without being healed? Second: Where exists such a heaven, off the earth, that flesh and blood can enter?[129]

Flesh and blood cannot survive without that of which it is made: the earth. Jesus' prophesy of the coming of the Son of Man is very clear, if you rightly understand. First: This removes all doubts in whom we should expect to execute judgment, for if man is to be judged and rewarded according to his actions, who could be justified in sitting as judge of man's doings but another man? How could a spirit be our judge when we cannot see a spirit? And, ever since life was created, life has had spirit. For without life there is no spirit. The Bible teaches that God will be seen on the Day of judgment. Not only the righteous will see Him, but even His enemies shall see Him.[130]

THE TRUE HISTORY OF MASTER FARD MUHAMMAD

A Saviour Is Born Chapter 5

As-Salaam-Alaikum

IN THE NAME OF ALLAH, THE MOST MERCIFUL, TO WHOM PRAISE IS DUE FOREVER, THE LORD OF THE WORLDS.

Brothers and Sisters, I'm so happy to see your smiling faces, who have come here from far and near to help us to give thanks to Almighty God, Allah, Who came in the Person of Master Fard Muhammad, To Whom Praises is due Forever.

A Savior's Day! Think about what we are here to worship. A Savior's Day! Who is Lost that we had to have a Saviour's Day?

I am a very happy man. A little small atom. I'm so small, you have to look for me, but if you keep your ears open, you will hear me. We have lots of people who are making our Saviour's Day worship one of the most beautiful ones I ever saw. Coming in, we saw just a wall of believers and our people who are seeking to learn just what a Saviour's Day looks like. We have plenty people in this country, millions of them, who would be here if they understood as you and me. Think over what day we're saying we worship. A Saviour's Day!

89

Had been lost so long that it has taken One Who loved us. It has taken One Who was made for us, out of the two people, to come and seek and find us. After finding us, he had to have the power to save and deliver us.

This Man had to be prepared. He was not already made and formed. He had to be prepared into a form to get among us. He could not come as He was: in the spiritual form of the Nation's mind.

So, His father had to prepare this Man to come and find us, then take us from our captors. We had been taken. This is why He, Himself, had to come. "Even I..." said the prophet; "...I will go after them. I will search the earth until I find them." A great lover with all power and with the eye to search the earth to locate that lost one.

We are a very beloved people for God, Himself, to come and search the Earth and the Nations to find we who were lost. We are greatly loved by God, Himself, to come and search the Earth for us. That's a beloved people.

He's so greatly in love for His people, that He threatened the whole population of the Earth to give them up. He said to me, that if you had been here in the days of Muhammad (may the peace and blessings of Allah be upon him), he would have come and got you himself.

That shows how important you are, that God will not allow one of us to be lost. Not to mention hundreds or thousands, but not one should be lost. He prepared Saviours to come for you. He says, in the Bible, "I will send Saviours after you."[131]

We are that important in the eyes of God and in the eyes of His angels, that He will send Saviours. He will send a whole host of them after you. They shall gather you from the West and bring you again into your own.

This is the day. A Saviour's Day! One born on this day - think over that - to save this poor lost people who have been lost from their own for over four hundred years.

"Even I," He says, "I will go." ...not send, but "I'm going myself."

As some of us know that this has been practiced under, secrecy, for a long time. But, today, He has arrived. Not King Solomon, but God, The King.

We are going to get over to you the History of This Man, Who is The Almighty God in Person, as He gave it to me.

He said to me, at the beginning His History, which I want you to listen carefully to, that His father was a Blackman, very much so, and His mother was a white woman.

He said that His father knew he could not be successful in coming to a solid white country, and he being a solid Black man. So, He taught me that His Father said, "I will go and make me a Son. And I will send my Son among them, looking like them." Think over that! "My Son, they will think He is one of them, and He will find our lost people."
So, Almighty God, in the Person of Master Fard Muhammad, said to me that he said, "I will have to make one look like them." So, He said, His Father went up into the hills and there

he found him a wife, a white wife. He took her and made a good Muslim out of her.

I don't know about that fancy, that we have in Bible, that He casted seven devils out of the woman to make her fit for giving birth to this Man, The Saviour.

I am not going to argue with no theologian about it, because there is something in it to prepare a woman, who by nature, is born of the devil to give birth to a man destined to be the Ruler and God in Person of the heavens and the earth.

Naturally, He had to be careful in preparing His wife.

So, He taught me that He was taken by His Father, after He was born. They went looking for every good book or books that contained great words of wisdom spoken by great Kings and of all great people.

He said that He would get a word or two from this one and a word or two from that one, which was put away as a secret and he'd bring it and give it to Him. He paid the people high prices for such a word or two on the History of such-and-such man. So these things, He was in preparation for a long time.

Let's go back to the hills now. He said, His Father found a wife for Himself up in the hills. I am not going into that with you right now, about where the hills were at and what they are called. I won't go into that with you right now. Some day you will hear me tell you, but I want to be sure that when I tell you that those in the hills will welcome me to tell you.

We have from Him that His Father married this woman and that the first child she birth for him was a girl. And He said his father said, "Uhm, I missed that time!"[132] So, He said, he made another try and that was Him. He said He took special care of Him so that He may be sent among the Western people - the Caucasian people. Of course, their real name you have known. Their real name is the devil. He needed one of these devil people in order to complete [what He wanted].

This is not a mockery, for me to stand here and call the people the devil, because that's what they are. If any mockery should be done, it should be done of us. Since we had made or created them, then the God of the Black man should be responsible for the mockery. I want to give you the truth. They didn't make themselves. We made them!

Well then, you have no right to be saying that your product is no good. Well, if you made it no good, then don't blame that which you made for being no good, because you made it. I know I'm coming to you in a way that you didn't think about. We are here to tell the truth.

As you have it in the Epistles of Paul, in the Bible, he says there, concerning this same subject, "The clay said to the potter, "Why make me thus?"[133] Well that's right! If you are the potter, the clay was innocent until you formed it and made it into something else. If you make another piece of pottery that you made mock of, you are the maker!

We must have understanding. We can't say that there was a mistake made and we should not recognize it. No. Listen at this good. I know you pretty well. The truth is truth. If one from among us made an enemy for us, we don't go after his product for doing it, we go after the maker. Why did you make us an enemy? He replies back to us, "to show what was in you. He was in you and you didn't know it. So I brought him out of you and made a form for him."

So He made the white race by taking them from us. As the Holy Qur'an challenges them after they had been given the power to rule, He reminds his creature, "Don't forget who made you, was it you, yourself, or was it we that made you?

This is to stop him from being proud over his maker, as though he had something to do with it. We are the only created people on Earth. The Black Man is a created man. The man that we call white, he is a made man from the Black man.

Since the white race was made from the Black Nation - the created people - what was the purpose of bringing out of the Black man that which he didn't know existed in him; something that could also be made a ruler if given a form. And if given the knowledge of the Black man, he could rule the Black man for a certain number of years until a greater one than he is produced by the Black man.

So this is what our Saviour, Master Fard Muhammad found in us. He came to save us, because we are a people who belong to the Creator. We are not a made people; I repeat, we are a created people; out of us, an unrighteous people were made, because we had that germ left in us from the creation of us. [This is] a germ that was not purified - one that we have in us today - whereas, it could be changed into a wicked germ.

Another people - a white people - could be made from us today, as we stand now. Regardless to how righteous we may be, we still contain the germ of unrighteousness. That is why we can do unrighteousness, because the germ is still there.

So, the great scientist by the name of Yakub, went after it. He brought it out of us and gave the germ a form - a body, and then taught that form his wisdom and told it - this made man - that he may, "Go forth now[134], be faithful, work fast, you got six days to do all of your work and after that six days, on the seventh day, the Brother coming from the East, he's gonna eat you up."

I want you to get a knowledge of this Saviour. That's what I'm working towards: His purpose, His aims. This is what I am trying to get over to you. I have got to bring you through history to get him to you.

He, Mr. Yakub - the mighty scientist and maker of the white race or white man - was no fool by any means, just because He made an enemy for us. This made us still great to know that in us was the germ of a whole race of people. We could form him and teach him, then make him rule the teacher for a certain length of time, until the people produced one greater than he.

A Saviour is born out of the germ, out of the plunder, out of the human scrap patch, He is made out of that. He's made partly from the race of Yakub and partly from His own, just for the purpose of saving you and me. A Saviour's Day it is rightly called. If we are so beloved, if we are so great a child, out of the family of the Creator, Who created the heavens and earth, should He let an enemy hold his child? Think over that. "No! I will go after him, search My own earth for him and I will bring him, again, to Me."

95

THE TRUE HISTORY OF MASTER FARD MUHAMMAD

What are you gonna do now, Father?" "I'm gonna clear this mistake so it will never happen again. There will never be a robbing or stealing away of some of our people, some of our own, by our enemies. No more! They won't be able to do so, for you are being taught the knowledge of the enemy. How then can he steal you after knowledge? How can he deceive you after knowledge? It can not be done.

We were so beloved, that God saw that He had to make a Savior for us. In the Bible, it says, He sent Saviour's after us. Think over that. He Sent Saviours - lots of Saviour's - to gather you from the hands of your enemy.

This has been a grievous thing. Just the idea that God has a child being held by an enemy, whom He has power over. Should He let them remain there, since they're only a few? No! Not even one! He will forgive you of your sins and then save you from the hands of the enemy, who made you sin after they robbed you of the knowledge of self. They made you follow and obey them in evil so that they could have us for a mockery before the All Wise and Holy God, Allah.

He has the power to take and forgive you, because it is not a sin of ours. It's a sin that we were practicing, because we couldn't help ourselves from our enemies. We were reared by enemies of ours and not friends. They deprived us of the knowledge of ourselves and of themselves. When he made us dead to the knowledge of ourselves, he then called us by his names. Now he goes to war to keep you from getting into your own: your own names. He don't want you "Mr. Muhammad". He wants "Morehouse". He wants "Moore", which is not a holy name. He calls you out of your name and calls you by his name. And as long as you go in his name, you belong to him.

You will soon see in a few days. If you come up with his name, then you'll go with him, because you rightly, then, belong to him. Since you refuse yourself and you're already with him, then you go on to hell with him.

This race of people - the white race - was not made to be saved. Some of them will live, though, for a long time, many centuries, those who have accepted Islam. There are many more of them that still await their turn to acknowledge Islam. They are coming into Islam, now, very fast, because they know the day they are living in and the time. You couldn't blame them. If I were in their place, you'd wake up looking at me and you would retire at night looking at me. I wouldn't never leave your house, because this is a race of people to be destroyed and not given another chance to deceiving the people.

There will be some that stick around maybe a thousand years, but they can't go beyond a thousand years even if they have believed, they can't go beyond the thousand years.

I won't go into no more of that, but that is true.

The Black man, He created heaven and earth and now comes to make a man. That's a small thing for Him to do, to make a man, when He had taken one atom out of the total darkness of the universe and made Himself.

We should be happy that we are Black people! He made it so clear that He did not allow a child to be born unless that child is born out of total darkness. This is following up on His Creation. Whether you are Black, white, red, brown or any color, you have got to be born out of total darkness to get on

97

this side. So therefore, He made his word "Be" stand and be steadfast; whereas, we can't move about in the darkness nor light unless we give Him credit.

I want you to love Black, because you are the universal God of all life. Regardless to what color it may be, originally it was made by the Blackman. There is no argument coming to you and me from the scientists of white people, that you are not the original man of the Earth.

Their scientists know this, because we have our mark on them. They couldn't deny it if they tried, if they know how to go into it.

We are the people to look toward when it comes to the making of the heaven and earth, as we are going to do it. At least...I'm not saying that I'm going to do it, but I'm helping now. This is why you're repeatedly hearing something about the beginning. How it was done. If you have caught up with the wisdom of that First Man, then it needs a second man to change the whole thing around, because you are not supposed to be standing aimless...No.
After the first God, we are practically now peeping into some of His art work, and finding in the root of this art work, a way to change up the whole thing. This is why, again, it is promised to you and me: a new heaven and a new earth.

Some of us say that it is spiritual. Yes, it is, at the present time. I bear witness, but it will be real one of these days, because this One, being equal in the knowledge to the first One, is capable of building Him a new one. As the Holy Qur'an teaches us, He can remove this one and build a new one, because He doesn't have to get a carpenter's tool. His word is sufficient.

We are trying to tell you more about this great architect - human architect. He's so great, as I said a minute or so ago, that His word is Be and you change from that. He doesn't have to go through the hard labor that Yakub went through to make a white people. His word is sufficient. And you start changing from The Word. This is why that just by a touch of His wisdom, you and me, we begin to change.

You are a great people, who have been called out of your name. Now God comes to prove that you are great. To the dissatisfaction of our enemy, he doesn't want to be exposed, but he knew for a long time his exposer was coming.

Today he accepts his exposure and does not argue with it, because he has had quite a few years to be ready for this day. He has a Bible that he translated, teaching him of his exposer and they are not dumb to it. It is you, the ones who were kept dumb, you and me! Just think of the idea of the Great Creator having His own people kidnapped by a made creature, made from Him. The race is a made race.

This is why you should not accept calling yourself a "race." YOU ARE A NATION! Not to think over a Negro or Colored people. This is mockery of you. It is mockery of you to call yourselves Mr. Jones and Mrs. Jones.

How could the white people, after being made to rule you and me until the coming of this Just One, teach us our own religion? How could he rule under our religion? Because if he had ruled us under Islam, then he would have been our brother; however, since he had to build a world for himself, he must not touch our world. He kept it away from us and he prepared him a false religion, then made you drink it.

He knows his religion is false. He knows he's false when he says, "Jesus Christ is the God. Jesus Christ will save us." He knows he is lying, because Jesus Christ is dead - the one he represents. But there is a new Jesus Christ! We are very happy to have this privilege of letting the Word come into the hearts of our people.

The Teachings, that He has raised me up from among you to teach to you, I will give you $10,000.00 at any time out of my brother's vest pocket, if you can find one of these words untrue. There has never been a preacher, regardless to what denomination or even his father - the Pope of Rome - able to give you a thorough knowledge of yourself and them too. This man was never before you before, that could back up his word with a high price. I could say a million as good as I can say ten thousand, because you will not be able to win.

He goes up in the mountains to make a wife for Himself, to get from her a Son that He could use under disguise[135] to get among the enemies and His people, and learn what was going on against His people.

I remember once He and I were talking. He said to me, "Brother, do you remember how they lynched that poor brother out there in Indiana over a false charge saying that he had raped a white woman?" I think that was in '30 that this happened. I said, "Yes sir. I read about it." He said, "Wasn't that a shame!" He said, "The women stood up on the tops of automobiles while the man was being lynched, yelling out to the lynchers, "Lynch that nigger!" Think over it! How many times we have been mocked and criticized with such names in the South. "Kill that nigger!" "Teach that nigger a lesson!"

I'm happy to say to you, a Saviour has been born to save us from our deadly rattlesnake, cobra-like enemy, [He is] a wild lion in the jungle, loose, day and night destroying our people. I want to say to you again and again, a Saviour has been born. If you are so foolish that you don't recognize and respect having a Saviour, today, stick around!

It is written in the History of Noah that when he closed the door of his boat they said, "Oh..." - knocking on his door when the water got up - "...Noah open unto us!" He said, "I can't." The Bible says they will say to you on This day "open unto us...", Asking the Saviour, "Was not we with you in the street?" But He'll say, "I know you not!"[136]

He declares that He don't know you if you are not a Believer. He means, that He don't know you as one to be saved by Him. You go with those, as the Bible says, who were in iniquity. You go along with them. The Holy Qur'an says "O...", they will say, "...would that I had taken a way with The Apostle after it had came to me." Meaning the Truth. "I let the enemy deceive me."[137] This is bad.

You are living in the Judgment Now! This IS the Judgment, and we are trying to separate you from that which God came to destroy, because you have no right to go along with them when you don't belong to white people. You belong to yourself! You are an independent people - created from the Nation of free people.
You don't need to go nowhere, but to yourself. There will be a Great Separation. It is on Now! As the Bible teaches you,

when you see people being called by the Names of God in your midst, having His mark, that's the Day of Resurrection and The Great Separation. You must be separated.

Ignorant people, having not the knowledge of the scriptures of the Bible, they will say to you, "Why separate?" That's a lover of the enemies and they don't want to be separated, but they will be separated against their will!"

The Holy Qur'an teaches us, that on that day, you that have made friends with the enemy will wish that the distance between you and them was the distance between the East and the West. To tell you the truth, you begin wishing that as soon as you know yourself.

You that are running around wanting to integrate and marry with them, that won't stand! As the Bible teaches you, your agreement with Hell will not stand.[138] You thought by marrying with the enemy, who holds power over you, you would be getting into that power, but you are not! He is careful to keep you out of that power. There is many of our people in Washington, some of them are now entering into the Cabinet. He will let them have a seat close to him. Yes sir. Just for them to help the white man destroy you, to keep you here.

A Saviour is Born!

Who is it that needs to be saved? It's you and me! You don't belong here, but an enemy has you tied by legal right of the law; therefore, you've got to break loose yourself in order to get free again. Wonderful!
So this man worked hard trying to make for Himself a Son to come and save us - a people who were out of the family and

out of the society of their own better people; so the God of the people goes to work to make for them a Saviour. This is wonderful!

So, on this day, February 26, we are faced with the truth that today we can say that the Man that was born 1877, February 26, is here with us to do what? To save us! This is wonderful!

To save us from what? From the destruction of our enemies, whom He has declared, with an oath, that he will deliver you from and destroy, those who has destroyed you.

Sometimes we make a mistake. Not an error, but make a mistake. Sometimes, as we are reaching out for more, we are forgetting that which we have already learned and counting it inferior to what we see before us.
We are being taught the Wisdom of this World, how one of our great scientist, sitting down playing with two pieces of steel, discovered the birth of a Nation. He could give birth to and teach them his wisdom and then make them rule us for six thousand years, until the Great Mahdi, Allah in Person, makes His appearance.
This has been done! Now, The Great Mahdi is here! Now He's ready to erase the kingdom of Yakub and build a people in the kingdom that will stand forever.

The people to whom we have been bowing (think over it) don't have anything to boast of. Ask them, who made them? They will say, "God." Then you ask them, "Who is God?" - They have deceived the slave and the slave's people all over the Earth concerning God and the heavens - He'll look up in the sky. You ought to tell him, say, "You don't look like a sky-born baby. You look like a baby born on the Earth." He knows you're too dumb to argue with him, but bring him here. We will argue with him.

He went to work, after he brought us from our native land and people, to make a mockery out of us, but he has as yet, done anything as great as Our Father did for him in the hills and cave sides of Europe, making monkeys and apes out of him. He made him grow animal tails, (think over that) and they still tell me, around hospitals, that some come here with little monkey tails. The monkey is his relative. Only one is civilized and the other one is uncivilized.

That's a curse which our people put on those of the devils who refused to listen to Moses. They made him a monkey; made him eat swine's flesh. He's called apes and swine in the Qur'an. He loves swine. Though you read in the Bible, you so-called good Christians, not only shouldn't you eat swine, but you shouldn't touch his carcass.[139]

You raise up your head and tell God, "What's wrong with it?" Talking back to the Man Who made it. They made the hog, not for the hog to be eaten. No! They made the hog to get the poison out for making medicine capable of reaching the white man's diseases. And he still uses that hog for his medicine. You saw in the papers or heard over the radio, about them using the hog. Some of them even want to plaster hog flesh on you.

He knows you don't like it. He does that for evil. Yes sir. You are told to put a piece of hog to your body. He knows the God would not like welcoming you in the Kingdom with a piece of forbidden flesh, of His own forbidding, on you.

So when they go to talking about, "I must put some hog flesh on you, that's best." Tell them, "No! If there is no other flesh, let me go ahead." There is enough poison pork worms into one square inch of the hog to kill you. You sit down dining with it and say, "It's good." As soon as that flesh gets inside of you, it starts creating members of it's family by the millions. Yes, this causes sickness.

The white man's drugs that he's preparing for you over the old drugs, it is only to make you die faster. I'm only telling you the truth. They will bear me witness.

A Saviour is Born! Who needed a Saviour any worse than we. We need a Saviour! You are hurting and in pain asking for help, asking for a drug to help you to bear your pain. He gives you a drug that will create another pain. This is true. He won't tell you to go and pray to Allah and try and help you. No, because he didn't serve Allah, and since he didn't serve Allah, he can't look to Allah for cures.

"Well, Muhammad, do you go to the doctor? Do you have pain? Are you sick?" IN ALL OF THEIR AFFLICTIONS, HE WAS AFFLICTED, BUT THE PLEASURE OF ALLAH WILL PROSPER WITH HIM (think over that).

You shoot off your mouth trying to make a mock of me. How can a man retrieve the drowning man? He doesn't have a boat to go out there, nor a bayou to put around his neck; so, he has to leap in there and battle the water and suffer as he suffers. This is what I'm doing. I am battling that which you battle. This shows the love of me for you. If God makes the man go through all of your suffering, it is to approve His choosing, to let you know that, "I chose one who loves you like I love you,

105

myself, and that he's willing to go through even death to lead you out of the hands of the enemy."

I could be living in Asia, in Africa, anywhere in the Western world or out of the Western world, because I am the brother of the righteous. Don't think that I suffer because I can't help myself or I am condemned by sin to be suffering with you. I am condemned by no sin that I have committed, because I have not sinned. Show me the history of any prophet of the past. I'm A Messenger. Show me their history and see if one escaped mockery of the people.

They all were mocked and accused of the evil of which he was trying to rid the people. If the last prophet must cover and fulfill the prophets before him, should not he go through with what he see the people going through until he can reach their hearts? He is a wise last prophet. He lived with you in your midst, then, after living with you and humbling himself to the same that you are buckled to and can't get out of, helps you unleash yourself from that which you cannot. Should then he be mocked? Regardless to what you put on me, I still have proof that I am fulfilling something that you probably didn't learn.

The Bible says, AFTER ELIJAH, THERE IS NO MORE PROPHETS. Why? He covers everything that a prophet has done or could do, if he was present, and brings you face to face with God and the devil that you no more need to be taught. "Here. Go there and you will learn about God." Stand still, brother, you will learn! No more shall they say that, "Here is the Lord" or "Here He is — over there in the desert." No more! "For they, all, shall know Me", He says.[140]

Our children are learning Who God Is so fast that they are out teaching other little children Who God Is. Sometimes you will find them with an audience of grown-ups, teaching them Who God Is. No more shall you say that, because "They all shall know Me." This is a wonderful day. A wonderful day!

We must know God! We cannot be saved from the enemies that we are bound to without the knowledge to the Real God. We are teaching you God in reality, not in a formless way. A formless God cannot teach form! You will run from a formless God and say you saw a spirit, and I think if you saw anything, it would have had to be that.

No more shall you teach the people that God is a spirit and that you have to die to see Him. You don't see nothing after you die. If you have seen anything after you died, where did they bury you at.

There is no coming back. After we die, there's no coming back! That's the end of all life: death. I DON'T CARE WHAT KIND OF LIFE IT IS, WHEN IT DIES, THAT'S THE END.

A Saviour is Born to teach us the knowledge of how to become self-saviours. When a man has the knowledge of himself, he's a self-saviour.

Almighty God, Allah, taught me that there isn't any such thing as death set as a boundary that you cannot pass. You kill yourself. That is true. We kill ourselves. No set time, brothers and sisters who are hearing this, that we have just got to die, because we live our time out. We live our time out when we are not able anymore to hold that time with the way to live.

107

THE TRUE HISTORY OF MASTER FARD MUHAMMAD

A plant sits out there as long as you water, nurse and cultivate the soil around it. It will live a long time. The water is the life of the plant and your cultivating it is the refreshing of the life of that plant. So it is with us.

There is no set time. He has taught, that we have just got to die anyway. The way we live kills us. I teach you, in a book titled How To Eat To Live, by just learning what to eat.

Eating food keeps us here and, He taught me, it takes us away. And that's natural. That's the nature of what nature has given to us. If we are going to follow nature. then, alright. If we eat, that's nature, but eat the right food. How can we live eating poison to our blood and flesh. We can't live like that. I don't care how much drugs you may pour into your body, it will give out on you one of these days, and you must find a way to eat to keep the body there. You should not eat two and three meals a day. You should not eat rough food that you feed beasts and animals on. They are made, by nature, with digestive juices which will digest anything like what you see them eating. They'll eat your food. You nurse them well, they'll live long.

There is a little book, How To Eat To Live, you should purchase this book. It's good for you to study! Study the book and eat so that you can live long.

Some of the ignorant will tell you, "I've been eating hog all my life. My father and my grandfather ate it and they lived 75, 80, or 90 years." You tell them, "He did not get out of babyhood." Seventy-five, eighty, and ninety years is still a baby.

You read in the Bible where men live nearly a thousand years.[141] How about you living just a few years, not even 100 years, and talking about you are happy that you were able to see 75, 85, or 100 years. That's nothing! The whole Earth has been here for untold trillions of years and still stands. If our house has been here for untold trillions of years and still stands, I say to you, brothers, try and live a little longer.

God taught me that He has pictures of the Martian people, and the devil believes it, because they have come so near to looking at the surface of Mars to look for creatures on it. They believe that they are there. They are very wise, very skillful, so Allah taught me. They hear his planes coming. They could hide away. They live there on that planet 1000 of our Earth years, so he may have seen a plane from the Earth yesterday. If they don't want to be seen by you, they don't have to let you see them. That's the truth.

You have people on Mars! Think how great you are. Ask the white man if he has any out there. We have life on other planets, but he don't. Allah wouldn't let Yakub scatter him over the planets. He couldn't live on Mars if you put him out there. The gravitation and the atmosphere that upholds Mars will kill either one of us Earth people who try to live on it. We couldn't even take a drink of water on it. It would kill you. We couldn't eat a piece of it's vegetation. It would kill you.

So, we should be satisfied that we are on the planet, our home. Be satisfied. There is no other planet that you and I can live on. We may go there, but you better stay inside of that contraption you go there in. All the scientists will agree with me on what I'm saying. You can't live on no other planet but the one you're born on. This one!

THE TRUE HISTORY OF MASTER FARD MUHAMMAD

God didn't make His Universe so that life could be transferred from one planet to the other and it survives in the atmosphere of that planet. So don't think about going to a star to live on, but this "star."

There is much that Allah has taught me in respect of planets and lives on these planets that I could say to you. We have them in Lessons and courses, but not given to you with that kind of secret. You will get it after a while. The knowledge of all the life that's in the nine planets, or on them, of which the Sun is the master over.

You will come to know the life that is existing in your own home. This is our home reaching out nearly five hundred billion miles in space. This is ours. We've go to stay here, but we make this home. The circle of our home is a beautiful thing. Nine beautiful planets rotating around the Sun, and we are riding on one of them and it is the master mind of all of them. Very Beautiful! The knowledge of these things all came from a Saviour for us, Who was born on this day, now, somewhat, about 119 years ago. He has come and has taught us the knowledge of these thing that we, now, are listening to.

A Saviour is Born. We, being dead to the knowledge of ourselves and others, He came and was born for the purpose of saving us from the destruction of our enemy. This is what has happened. The time of the enemy is up! He lives as long as we are dead to the knowledge of self. A Saviour, today, in the Person of Master Fard Muhammad, to Whom Praises are due forever, has chosen us and, now, we choose Him to be our God and we His people.

So, in my conclusion, I say to you, remember on this day A Saviours was Born! Know that we have a Saviour to save us. A Saviour born to save us, who was destined for the destruction along with our enemies, but we, being lost among the enemy, a Saviour was made to come and save us. His father loved us and went to work to make a Man that would come among us under disguise so that the Bible may be fulfilled. "Behold! He cometh as a thief in the night, while men slept."[142] In that night (spiritual dark night) He found us. And He made ONE of us to go after the others when the Sun arises.

We had three years and nearly a half in the night, teaching me His wisdom - How to save you from the hands and power of the enemy.

I learned my Lesson well. I have not lost sight of it one hour. I'm here. If any of you wants to see God, wants to be saved, as He is The Saviour: Master Fard Muhammad, to Whom Praise is Due forever, then follow me.

So, as I say unto you, my beloved Saved Ones, for He said he would not lose one of us. The Bible says, symbolically referring to us, all Israel will be saved.[143] That don't mean white Israel.

If the Father of Master Fard Muhammad was so loving to us, whom He had not seen, let us make Him feel proud that we accepted His Son, because we want to be saved. Thank you brothers and sisters. Let us not forget that February 26, is The Saviour's Day!

THE TRUE HISTORY OF MASTER FARD MUHAMMAD

As-Salaam-Alaikum.

That Which You Should Know – Interpretation of Signs Chapter 6

We had not been known to be in this part of the earth until around 70 to 80 years ago or a little better. We had been swallowed up into the slavery of the American white man, who put us in his name and language. This absolutely hid us from our people's knowledge, resulting in their ignorance of our whereabouts, until the birth of the Great Messiah or The Mahdi, God in person, was born to find us. This knowledge is now universal, that we have been found and this finding of that lost member of the black nation of the earth, is today, what the whole entire resurrection and judgment of the world, the setting up of the kingdom of righteousness is about. They are the pillars or foundational stones of the kingdom of heaven, about which God has caused to be prophesied through the mouths of His prophets: that He will build upon the earth after the reign and rule of the present civilization of the Caucasian world.

We have been found, as I have foresaid, and the knowledge is now universal. We don't know that we are found, and that what Allah has revealed to us has gone around the earth into the ears of every wise scientist; especially, those scholars of the scriptures and prophets of the Holy Nation of Islam. They have heard of our findings and they realize that Almighty God Allah has appeared among us. There is no way possible that we could have been heard of or rise up into the knowledge of

113

God, into the knowledge of ourselves, or into the knowledge of the enemy of God, if God had not visited among us Himself in person to teach us this knowledge.

That there are signs that absolutely agree with everything that I'm saying. These particular truths have been kept from the ears and knowledge of their wisest scientists of all time, in order to bring it to pass as it should be. There was no actual real teachings of it; there was no real knowledge of where the lost members of our people would be found. There only was symbolic teachings of it.

Jesus referred to it in a parable, as in a wilderness; wherein, a man having 100 head of sheep and one of them went astray. He leaves the 99 and he goes after the one that goes astray; he goes into a wilderness. There he finds the sheep, brings him out again to join onto the 99, making the 100 full.[144] This refers to people and not to sheep, goats and animals, but actually it refers to people who's characteristics are similar to that of sheep and goats. The wicked is referred to as goats and the righteous as sheep; this is due to the characteristics of the two.[145]

The so-called American Negroes answer this description one hundred percent of the "lost-found" pictured by Jesus and by a few prophets in the Old Testament.

We have a parable made by Samson in the Old Testament with reference to a slain lion. Bees were making honey in the mouth of its carcass and an eagle came along and ate some of the honey out of the mouth of the carcass of the lion.[146] Remember, these parables and riddles have a great meaning of something to come in the future. Here, the lion represents a lion like people, a powerful people, a vicious people, an evil people. A young lion means a young vicious civilization or a young government of people that would be very vicious, but in that vicious and evil government, there would be something good there that should be taken out, and the only way that it can be taken out is to capture the young lion and destroy its power to hold and keep the prey that it has captured. The bees bringing honey into the carcass' mouth refers to good things coming from God by the angels, and this sweetness coming into the carcass represents the truth, and out of that truth, would come the carcass in his mouth. This would also be good for those people to eat. It represents the truth being born in such a condition of the world and people, that at the end of the world, the sign of the pilgrimage to Mecca, the Black Stone, being made, has been going on now for nearly the last 1400 years.

The Holy Qur'an refers to it and the Bible refers to it, but these are signs of the coming of a nation that was hidden and lost, which God Himself would go after in the last days. After finding that nation, choose that nation for Himself and take it and use it as a builder would in selecting stones or a foundation for a substantial building that he intends to build. He want to build it so it could withstand any strong winds or storms throughout eternity or as long as the earth lasts.

Stones from the earth that has good texture and will stand or live as long as the earth, is necessary in building an eternal kingdom upon the earth that will stand forever, which will not be destroyed by any opposition that may arise. These signs are used for it; the sign of a stone.

The True History of Master Fard Muhammad

In Daniel it is referred to[147] and in Jesus' prophesy of this people as a stone that the builders rejected, which had become the head and the corner.[148] This is none other than the people of whom the builders of civilization has rejected in the past. They will one day become the head and the corner building of a civilization which will supersede and become the strongest and the mightiest and the greatest of all the civilizations and people that ever was before it. This refers to the lost and found members, the original people who are now called the American Negroes. I wish everyone of you who are called Negroes would jump and shout on hearings of this truth of you.

You have the greatest future of anybody who ever lived on the planet earth, if you would only come and submit to Allah and follow me. This you can learn and enjoy, not having to wait a thousand years, not having to wait a hundred years to enjoy it, right now you can begin enjoying the kingdom of heaven; right now! The King of that kingdom is now present, and the King of that Kingdom is now selecting you for the foundation of that Kingdom; therefore, He says to you in these words: "Submit to me and I will sit you into heaven at once. Money, good homes - friendship in all walks of life." This is absolutely true as sunshine. There is lots of opposition against you receiving this salvation and enjoying heaven at once while you live from those who would like to see you to continue to live in the most miseries that humans have ever lived in since there was a man on the face of the earth.

I'm here as a brother, a friend to you, and one of the first from the resurrection. I am the very first. I am the first of those who submitted to the Will of God, in the person of Master Fard Muhammad, to Whom praise is due forever. I am the first. I am he of whom it is written that was dead and now alive.[149] I am he. I am he of whom it is prophesied as the Messenger of God in the last day who is with God in the resurrection of the dead. I am he. Let your ignorant enemy of the righteous and the truth deceive you against these truths, if you want to take such a one for your guide and for your interpreter. You will suffer the torment and hell of this life. The rejection of the Almighty God, today, and His Messenger will get you nothing but hell in this life, not after you are dead, but while you live.

Take for an instance, the pilgrimage to Mecca that has been going on for the last 1400 years. It is only a sign. Even the city itself is only a sign. Even the Kabbah, that mighty sign sitting there clothed with a black veil, is only a sign. The running to and fro between the hills and the ruins, while visiting this, and heard about in that way: depicts Abraham's wife, Haggar with her young son lying there in the heat suffering for water. He and her went in to find water there. She looked at the feet of her child and there was a well bubbling under her feet that would never go dry. It's only a sign of the coming of God and the finding of His people.

I'm the type of preacher who can hardly get the truth over to you without making such strong expressions, due to the spirit of God Who has found us, that I feel that I should force it to you. I should force it into your ears. With this truth, I will bring you into the knowledge of yourself and will set you in heaven at once; yet, you are making a grave effort of trying to succeed in getting into such enjoyment from those who have actually brought you into a hell of a condition. You are suffering under great sorrow and torches of death, trying to get this beautiful rest and peace of God, from your enemies and opposers of your salvation.

The True History of Master Fard Muhammad

Be wise and know the truth. These things which I continue preaching, you should know. It is the truth that will bring you into salvation and a heavenly life, which you have been longing for, for the past 400 years while in the Western Hemisphere.

Go into Mecca, making a pilgrimage to that city, as the 22nd Surah says to you and me in the 27th verse: It says to the Messenger here: "Proclaim to men the pilgrimage, they will come to thee on foot and on every lean camel coming from every little part or path." From all over the earth there has been pilgrimages made to this city. It is a sign that one day at the end of this world, the rule of Satan, the Messenger will call people from every direction, from all of the nations of the Blackman. This is the sign of the resurrection; whereas, whenever the real truth of God has been known, and made manifest to the world through the mouth of that Messenger in the resurrection, every human being who is originally of the nation or aboriginal nation of the earth, will come to the knowledge of that One God, the Truth and to the knowledge of that one shepherd or that one Divine Messenger in that day. Everyone will bow in submission to His will. As the Bible refers to it in this beautiful term, that, "Every knee shall bow, every tongue shall confess that He is God - besides He there is no God."[150]

In the ending of the Bible, that last book referred to as the Revelation of John, there we have a symbolic picture of God and the Lamb. The Lamb there receives the greatest revelation that any human beings have ever witness since the creation of the heavens and earth. He receives it directly from the All Wise God, Himself, a revelation that was denied the angels of heaven and given to a symbolic person symbolized as a sheep,

118

which only depicts the characteristics of that Last Messenger. The Last Messenger is a person that is despised and rejected. One of those members of that lost and found people, who were rejected and despised by the builders of civilization, now receives the greatest revelation of all time: to place the unwanted, unfit, rejected, despise, trampled, and murdered outcasts of civilization, into the love and mercy of Almighty God. The mercy of Almighty God and His love in making them His choice and His selection of this particular unwanted people, by the civilizations, would cause the nations of the earth to bow into submission for the first time, since the creation of the heavens and the earth, to that One God, and there, be united together as pilgrims. The sign of it represents or rather is a prophesy of the divine unity of the God and the people of ours and the God together. This doesn't mean divine unity between God and the enemy of God, it means divine unity of that people which is of God, who have not known that they were of God and who have not known that they were of the real members of God.

This is what we are to learn. This is what I want you to learn today: Today is the call for you to make a pilgrimage. Not a pilgrimage to Mecca for you to be sanctified or become a Holy Muslim. This will not make you a Holy Muslim: going to Mecca, making the pilgrimage there. Every so-called Negro in America can go if he wanted to or if he's able to, but will that make him the divine choice today? No, because this is a new thing coming in: the presence of God.

After 6,000 years of the work of an evil people, who have ruled the nations under evil and deceit, a very deceptive people, a people for whom the righteous labored under. They are a grievous and a very unjust government, who have poured upon

119

the righteous the worst that could be had or a man could labor under. Today the righteous are now called to make the pilgrimage. Make your last pilgrimage, not to that particular city, per say, looking for glorification as they have in the past. People in the past have worked and made the pilgrimage to Mecca and have returned to their people and teachers to teach them of this sign, but I say the American so-called Negroes are the end of that sign. A pilgrimage there [Mecca] will not help him become a great and righteous Muslim, but the bowing down to that Last Messenger, who God raised from the dead of that people, and recognizing him as being the Guide now for the dead or the absolute [one] to give life to that dead nation, bringing them forth to God, is the real Mecca to which they should make pilgrimage. The finding of this people and the choice of God for this people to be His, and making them the foundation, a stone for building the kingdom of heaven on earth, absolutely is the end of all pilgrimages. The sign will serve no more purpose when it has been fulfilled. Today, it's being fulfilled.

So here is where the Negro, the so-called Negro, the lost and found member of that righteous nation, must first bow and make a circuit. He must first make a self-confession and join the circle that God is making in the West, so he may be recognized in the circle of the East. This is where he must first pull off the old garments; this is where he must first put on a new coat and the new faith it represents. He must change clothes here, change faith, that's all it means; so he may enter into the mercy of Almighty God and see the hereafter, at which point the earth will become a whole Mecca; wherein, the nations of this earth, of Aboriginal people, will no more go to Mecca to worship there, but everywhere, as the Jesus prophesied, there would be Mosques in their hearts.[151]   As he

120

said to the woman there of Israel: "Woman believe me, the hour cometh", which means the doom of this world "... when ye shall neither in this mountain..." meaning the government of Israel "...nor yet at Jerusalem, the capital, worship the Father." "Ye worship what you know not what; we know what we worship: for salvation is of the Jews." Listen, let us see and understand what he's talking about. Not yet is this the place where ye shall worship, but the time of the doom after that. All men shall not seek to go no certain place, the whole earth will be a Mosque. The whole earth will be a mountain of God where man will worship Him in the spirit of truth and sincerity.

ENDNOTES:

1. Elijah Muhammad, Message To The Blackman In America, (Muhammad Mosque of Islam No. 2, Chicago, IL, 1965; p.243.
2. C.E. Lincoln, The Black Muslims in America, Rev. Ed., (Boston: Beacon Press, 1973), p. xxiii.
3. Ibid., pp. xxiii-xxiv.
4. A. Huff Fauset, Black Gods of the Metropolis, Negro Religious Cults of the Urban North, (Philadelphia: University of Pennsylvania Press, 1944), p. 107.
5. Ibid., pp. 107-8
6. Ibid., p. 121
7. J.M. Yinger, Religion, Society and the individual, (New York: The Macmillian Co., 1957), p. 504, as quoted in C.E. Lincoln, The Black Muslims in America, p. 57.
8. C.E. Lincoln, The Black Muslims in America, p. 57.
9. Ibid., p. 62.
10. Ibid., p. 61.
11. Ibid.,
12. It has not completely disappeared. The new name is the United Afro-American Improvement Association.
13. Martha F. Lee, The Nation of Islam, An American Millenarian Movement, Ewin Mellen Press: Lewiston/Queenston Lampeter, p.30-31
14. C.E. Lincoln, The Black Muslims in America, p. 14.
15. Sahib, Hatim. The Nation of Islam. M.A. Thesis, University of Chicago. 1951.
16. Ibid., p. 69.
17. Morroe Berger, The Black Muslims: Horizon Mag, 1961, vol. I.
18. Elijah Muhammad, History of The Nation, Secretarius Publications, Atlanta, p. 76-78.
19. Hakim Shabazz, Essays On The Life and Teachings of Master W. Fard Muhammad, UB & US Communications Systems, p. 11.
20. Ibid., p. 7
21. Drew Ali, The Holy Koran of the Moorish Science of America, p. 59; as quoted in Hakim Shabazz, Essays On The Life And Teachings of Master W. Fard Muhammad, p 7.

22. Hakim Shabazz, Essays On The Life And Teachings of Master Fard Muhammad, p. 7

23. Elijah Muhammad, Message To The Blackman In America, 1965, p. 21, 86 & 287.

24. Ibid., pg. 287.

25. Hakim Shabazz, Essays On The Life And Teachings of Master W. Fard Muhammad, p. 7.

26. Bible: 1 John 3:2.

27. Webster II, New Riverside University Dictionary; 1984, Houghton Mifflin Co.

28. Ibid.,

29. Bible: Isaiah 40:12.

30. Bible: Jeremiah 31:9

31. Bible: Ezekiel 2:1

32. St. John 5:26, 27.

33. Bible: Genesis 1:26

34. Bible: Matthew 24:27

35. Bible: Revelations 12:1

36. Elijah Muhammad, Messenger of Allah, The Flag Of Islam, 1974; pg. 30.

37. Bible: St. John 3:13.

38. Bible: Romans 5:12

39. Bible: Genesis 37:9

40. Bible: Revelations 21:23; 22:5

41. Elijah Muhammad, Message To The Blackman In America; Muhammad's Temple No. 2, 1965, pp. 19,20.

42. Paraphrasing a fictitious person.

43. Bible: Revelations 21:23.

44. Bible: St. John 10:16.

45. Bible: 1 Corinthians 15:22, 45-47

46. Holy 'Qur'an 15:28

47. Bible: St. Luke 17:20

48. Bible: Isaiah 63:3

49. Bible: Galatians 4:28, Hebrews 11:9

50. Bible: Revelation 12:14

51. Bible: Revelation 19:16. See also Messenger Elijah Muhammad, Theology of Time Lecture, Audio tape. June 4, 1972, Recorded in Chicago.

52. Elijah Muhammad, Message To The Blackman In America, Muhammad's Temple of Islam, No. 2, Chicago, IL, pg. 141.

53. Bible: Revelation 4:10-5:12

54. Bible: Revelation 21:3
55. Bible: Matthew 24:27.
56. Ibid., 24:30.
57. Elijah Muhammad, Message To The Blackman In America, Muhammad's Temple of Islam; No. 2, Chicago, IL, 1965, pg. 289.
58. Ali, Maulana Muhammad, The Holy Qur'an; translation, 5th ed., 1963: 4:163.
59. Bible: Isaiah 49:24-26
60. Bible: Luke 13:7.
61. Bible: II Thessalonians 2:9.
62. Bible: Revelation 3:12
63. Bible: Proverb 10:7
64. Bible: Ezekiel 34:11.
65. Bible: John 11:25.
66. Bible: Revelations 14:13.
67. Bible: Genesis 15:13.
68. Bible: Isaiah 43:5.
69. Bible: Ezekiel 17:22.
70. Bible; Genesis 15:13.
71. Bible: Deuteronomy 18:15-18.
72. Ibid., Isaiah 9:6 and 53rd chapter.
73. Ali, Maulana Muhammad, The Holy Qur'an, Chapters 3:41, 42,44, & 46.
74. Holy Qur'an: 43:59.
75. ibid., 23:50.
76. Bible: Matthew 1:19-20.
77. ibid., 1:18.
78. Bible: Mark 3:31-32.
79. Bible: John 19:38.
80. Bible: Romans 8:3.
81. Bible: Psalms 110:1
82. Bible: Ezekiel 25:12.
83. ibid., 21:7
84. Bible: Ezekiel 36:24.
85. Bible: Ezekiel 1:1,2,15,18.
86. Bible: St. John 14:16, 26; 15:26; 16:7
87. Here, [...like he sent me to these devils] Messenger Elijah Muhammad is paraphrasing the words of Jesus and not speaking possessively. I felt that it was necessary to make this very clear to the reader, because when reading this passage and not hearing the tone of this statement coming directly from

the Messenger could sometime produce misunderstanding. Based on the authority with which the Messenger spoke, he would exercise that authority by elaborating on what prophets or messengers of the past may or may not have meant in their statements. The Messenger would give the correct interpretation in its proper context.

88. On numerous occasions, the Messenger would talk as though he takes on the role of Jesus, stating what Jesus of 2000 years ago would state and knowing exactly what should have been stated in case the scriptural writers either failed to put it in their interpretation of the Bible or just didn't have the interpretation, which was and is generally the case. The point to keep in mind is that many have surfaced and have intentionally taken such phrases out of context for the purpose of putting the Messenger of today in Jesus' place of 2000 years ago thereby creating a vacuum for "another" to come after Messenger Elijah Muhammad - themselves!

89. Bible: Deuteronomy 18:15, 18.
90. Bible: Jeremiah 31:33.
91. Bible: John 1:18
92. Bible: John 3:13
93. Bible: Matthew 2:1
94. Bible: Acts 1:9-11
95. Bible: St. Luke 2:16
96. Elijah Muhammad, JESUS: His Birth, Death And What It Means To You And Me, Secretarius Publications, pg. 33, 1st edition 1993.
97. Ibid., pg. 33
98. Bible: Matthew 1:18; St. Luke 1:27; 2:5.
99. Holy Qur'an 23:50.
100. Bible: John 8:44.
101. ibid., 8:42.
102. ibid., 8:39.
103. Holy Qur'an 43:59.
104. Holy Qur'an 5:111-118.
105. Bible St. John 5:30.
106. ibid., 20:17.
107. ibid., 17:11-12.
108. Bible: St. Luke 16:20.
109. Holy Qur'an 3:48.
110. Bible: St. Luke 1:57.
111. Bible: St. Luke 2:14.
112. Bible: Matthew 24:7-10.
113. ibid., 10:34.

114. Bible: Malachi 4:5-6.
115. Bible: St. Luke 14:26.
116. Bible: Romans 9:13.
117. Bible: Exodus 2:2.
118. Holy Qur'an 21:92.
119. ibid., 19:17.
120. Holy Qur'an 7:113-114.
121. Holy Qur'an 19:88-93.
122. Bible: Matthew 1:20-21.
123. ibid., 1:16-20.
124. ibid., 1:23.
125. Bible: Matthew 9:6.
126. ibid., Matthew 24:27,30,37,39,44.
127. Bible: Matthew 25:36.
128. Bible: Matthew 24:37-39.
129. Bible: 1 Corinthians 15:50.
130. Bible: 1 John 3:2.
131. Bible: Nehemiah 9:27.
132. Here, we see that even Allah, (God), Lord and Master of the Creation, submits to the natural course of His own law. This helps us understand the serious gravity of the false claim that God had gotten Mary pregnant with Jesus our of wedlock, which would be a violation of the law of marriage. God does not violate His own law then expects us to submit to them.
133. Bible: Romans 9:21.
134. Bible: Genesis 1:28.
135. Bible: Romans 8:3.
136. Bible: St. Luke 13:25.
137. Holy Qur'an: 25:27. Also see Message To The Blackman In America, by Elijah Muhammad, pg. 294-296.
138. Bible: Isaiah 28:18.
139. Bible: Deuteronomy 14:8.
140. Bible: Jeremiah 31:34; Hebrews 8:11.
141. Bible: Genesis 5:27.
142. Bible: I Thessalonians 5:2.
143. Bible: Romans 11:26.
144. Bible: St. Luke 15:4.
145. Bible: St. Matthew 25:32-33.
146. Bible: Judges 14:8.
147. Bible: Daniel 2:35.
148. Bible: St. Mark 12:10.

149. Bible: St. Luke 15:24,32.
150. Bible: Isaiah 45:23; Romans 14:11.
151. Bible: St. John 4:21-22.

Thank you for purchasing this book.
We trust the reading was rewarding and enlightening.
We offer various titles and a comprehensive collection of
Messenger Elijah Muhammad's works.

These works include:

- Standard Published Titles
- Unpublished & Diligently Transcribed Compilations
- Audio Cassettes
- Video Cassettes
- Audio CD's
- DVD's
- Rare Articles

You are welcomed to sample a listing of these items by simply requesting a FREE archive Catalog.

Our Contact information is as follows:

Secretarius MEMPS Ministries
111 E Dunlap Ave, Ste 1-217
Phoenix, Arizona 85020-7802
Phone & Fax 602 466-7347
Email: secmemps@gmail.com
Web: www.memps.com

Wholesale options are also available.